The Sasquatch People

The Sasquatch People

Guardians of the Earth

Memoirs of a Sasquatch Experiencer

Leanna R Saylor

DAGMAR
MIURA
LOS ANGELES

Published by Dagmar Miura
Los Angeles
www.dagmarmiura.com

The Sasquatch People: Guardians of the Earth

This book is a memoir. It reflects the author's present recollections of experiences over time. Certain names have been changed to maintain the individuals' anonymity.

The photographs of old growth forest on the front and back covers were taken by the author in the Olympic National Park, Washington State. All drawings were created by the author.

First published 2023

ISBN: 978-1-956744-84-2

I dedicate this book to Mannie, the Sasquatch elder who stepped forward and connected me to his Sasquatch family and community.

Contents

Introduction

I HAVE DECIDED TO tell my story about the ongoing experiences and interactions I have been having with a species of humans whom I believe are the Sasquatch People. I consider myself to be what is called a Sasquatch experiencer, someone who is having experiences and contact with Sasquatch.

For the sake of clarity, when I write Sasquatch, I will always write it singularly as such, Sasquatch, even if more than one Sasquatch are being referred to. When I learned about Sasquatch, I heard it used in the singular form. I have never heard nor read Sasquatch used in the plural form, i.e., Sasquatches. Therefore, in keeping with the custom to which I was introduced to, I will always make this reference in the singular form: Sasquatch.

Many years ago, when I first heard about Sasquatch, it was from Native Americans. I learned to pronounce Sasquatch as *Suss-kwatch;* this is how I have always heard this name spoken by Native Americans. I feel their enunciation is correct and should be acknowledged, respected and used accordingly.

SASQUATCH EXIST ALL OVER the world. With frequency, they have been sighted in the United States, especially in the Pacific Northwest Region. I would like to add that they are invisible, unless you know how to see them, or unless they materialize into physical form. When asked, "What do you call yourselves?" They answer, "Guardians of the Earth."

During the early stages of my relationship with Sasquatch, I decided to write a book about them, who they are, and what they stand for. I have done just that, and everything I have written is described to the best of my ability with great attention to detail. This story represents my interpretation of a series of ongoing events that I cannot explain. To have encounters with Sasquatch is to enter the arena of "high strangeness."

Sasquatch are inter-dimensional beings that live in the fourth dimension. They can move between the fourth dimension and our third-dimensional plane easily. However, for the most part, they spend their time in the fourth dimension, where I have concluded the quantum physical field exists. Their daily lives are based on quantum physical laws unfamiliar to us human beings living with earth-bound laws like gravity, time and space to name a few. At times during the story, I will refer to their power and abilities as "paranormal." In their world, the daily norm is to be able to perform what might appear to us as magic. Yet, for Sasquatch it is not magic. It is just part of their everyday existence.

There is no scientific evidence to prove the existence of Sasquatch. However, there is abundant physical evidence gathered by professionals who have scientifically documented their findings such as footprints, hair samples and examples of their massive tree trunk sculptures built for the purpose of marking territory deep in the forests. These incredible sculptures are enormous and could not be replicated by man without the aid of heavy equipment. The tree trunks used in these markers are torn out of the ground and woven back and forth intricately between other tree trunks equally as massive that have been harvested in like manner. Yes, there is much proof that something does exist in the forests, particularly the forests of North America and Canada.

The fact that these forms of evidence are physical in nature, combined with thousands of reported sightings, is legitimate proof for me of their existence. The premise on which scientific proof is currently based requires a corpse for evaluation before receiving the scientific stamp of approval, "Okay, you do exist, but now, you are dead. Sorry about that."

This practice needs upgrading to fit in with the level of sensitivity our population has willingly elevated itself to. These methods lack ethics towards living matter other than human beings. Most of us can no longer tolerate the practice of killing, poisoning or polluting any living plant, mammal, river, ocean or even Sasquatch in our world today. We are better than that. We have become much more enlightened. We can be better, way better.

Be that as it may, Sasquatch are becoming more and more recognized by people worldwide through personal encounters like mine. To be in contact with Sasquatch is to begin the journey of restoring your life, the lives of your loved ones, the lives of your friends, the world, and so forth, and so on.

The Sasquatch hope many humans will welcome the personal growth and development they offer freely. We have an opportunity to watch personal evolutionary changes take place within ourselves and within our lifetime. They are ready to help us human beings improve our lives for the better. Who knows, they just may well become our next rock stars!

Chapter One

Two Abandoned Kittens Find a Home

M Y HUSBAND JERRY AND I started up a general contracting company in the year 2001. We worked hard doing tenant improvements and remodels of all kinds in commercial spaces such as dental offices, real estate offices, restaurants and more. For the most part, the bulk of our work was done at the local hospital, upgrading and improving numerous patient care units of all kinds.

I took charge of all the bookkeeping and management of the office, ran errands, managed the fleet of trucks and work vans and was on call whenever something was needed at any time of day. Jerry's time was spent working seven days a week, keeping up with a demanding schedule. He kept the crew working full-time. For the most part, Jerry got his work through word of mouth. We worked hard and were somehow able to keep up with the endless details involved with running a small contracting business. Invariably, there were ups and downs, believe you, me.

When we started the company, we were renting a small house in town. In 2004, we moved out to the county after our rental home went up for sale. The house in the county was a hundred years old and situated on a quarter-acre of land. The area in the county was very tranquil, with wide views of the sky by day and the stars by night. We had no neighbors, and so we settled in excitedly with great anticipation about life in the county and all that it entailed. We were also interested in the wildlife and wondered what kind of critters lived in the area. Both Jerry and I loved nature.

In the distance, our property was surrounded by old, dilapidated farms. There were fields covered with remnants of old fencing along the gently rolling, hay-covered hills. These had been farms from long ago. Rusty bits of barbed wire fencing and rotting cedar fence posts lay strewn about here and there around the abandoned fields.

Near our house stood a short row of towering Lombardy Poplars jutting up around a silvery pond edged with cattails. In summer, the pond was covered with white water lilies. When we took walks around the pond after work in the early evening, we entered an enchanted world, a mystical realm reclaimed by nature and forgotten by time, where frogs, fish, dragonflies and different bird species thrived. The pond was their home, and it was magical. We visited it often.

Each spring, hundreds of green tree frogs filled the cold night air with a wondrous chorus of croaking that echoed far across the fields. Their music could be heard far and wide throughout the night, marking the end of winter and the promise of spring. We considered our new home a "piece of heaven."

ONE DAY IN 2006, we adopted a lost male kitten that turned up on our property hungry and in need of a home. He was a short-haired, black and gray blotched tabby with astonishing markings, unlike any I had ever seen. He resembled a wild species of cat that lived in the jungle trees.

We called him Feller. I spent a great deal of time training him, and he became a member of our family. He spent his days following me everywhere I went. We played together each day inside the house with cat toys, and we created a tight bond. I became not only his friend but also his mother. We were inseparable. One day, when I decided he was large enough and old enough to have good sense, I let him go outdoors. I was cautiously aware of the coyote pack that passed through our area occasionally. Every night he slept with me on our bed. I had always been closely bonded with cats, but this cat was different. He was something special, and I swear he knew what both Jerry and I were thinking and feeling. He paid good attention to us both. He was my baby, and I was his Mom.

Feller grew big and very strong. We thought he may have been an American Shorthair, as he demonstrated excellent skills associated with the breed. They are known to be aggressive mousers, and he indeed found the right property for a home, as rodents were not in short supply. Over time, we received numerous hunting trophies, which he left behind for us on the porch: shrews, moles, house mice, field mice and different species of rats. Feller turned out to be a voracious hunter and cleaned out the mice and rats in our surround. He did his job well, and we respected him for it. He had his place in our family. We came to depend on him for rodent control. He was very loyal, affectionate and attentive to us both.

As a big cat weighing in at 16 pounds with steel claws, he

lorded over our property protectively. He was solid and powerful, and he carried himself as such. On the other hand, his personality was somewhat like a faithful dog in that he came whenever he was called. He usually came running with bright eyes full of anticipation with a big, cat grin. We knew we had a special cat living with us. We were a happy and contented family of three. Life just could not get any better.

THINGS WERE GOING WELL for the three of us. We were all working and enjoying what life had to offer. We were secure. Then one afternoon, six years later, a ten-month-old, orange-striped tabby kitten with white socks, a white tuxedo and a white-tipped tail turned up on the porch. He was yowling mournfully, covered with dirt and fleas and was frightfully thin. It was apparent he had not eaten for quite a while. All his rib bones were protruding and could be counted one by one. He behaved traumatized and disenchanted. He was the unhappiest kitten I had ever seen. I adopted him at once.

I began feeding him small meals all day long, as I was concerned about the state of his digestive tract. I kept a bowl of fresh water and a soft bed for him on the porch. His eyes betrayed his lost innocence as a kitten. Grief-stricken, he began returning for the food, water and bed. Over time, he finally understood that it was all for him, and he decided we would be safe and okay. I told the kitten, "You are home. We are your family now, and we want you here with us." It seemed to me that he was listening.

Feller did not find the newcomer a threat but rather watched with great interest while I attended to the needs of this sad, abandoned kitten. In my heart and mind, I reassured him that he would never go hungry again and would be safe and loved. He was with his real family now, where he belonged. We would never abandon him.

The mother hen in me shifted into high gear. My job would not be done until this lost animal was fully restored. My goal for him was optimal health, quality of life, love and happiness in this world. I was ready to protect him from the whole world single-handedly.

The first order of the day was to get a clean bill of health from our veterinarian. It took several appointments with our house-call veterinarian to get him up to speed on vaccinations and to get rid of ear mites, worms, and the like. We planned to have him neutered, once he was old enough and was settled into his new life here with us.

The kitten proved to be very gentle and well-behaved. He liked being inside the house, so I allowed him to live indoors regularly with us. I looked forward to him finding his place within our family. When the veterinarian completed all the necessary medical work and health upgrades, he told the kitten, "You are a lucky cat!" I sensed this was a lucky cat, but I also felt many other cats were not so fortunate, a sad and discouraging thought.

The steady, good meals were erasing the deep creases between his ribs, and he was growing longer and taller. It appeared he would be a larger cat than Feller. Slowly, his outlook on life changed, and he became more trusting of his new situation. It was the right time to give him a name. He was a graceful animal and seemed like royalty. We named him Prince. We could see he was part Abyssinian with the classic long ears, long neck and long nose. He was regal, alright—he was a Prince. His impressive Roman nose and prominent ears stood straight up in perfect unison with the other fine feline features of his head, giving him the appearance of a show-quality cat. He was "our" show quality cat, our trophy cat! I was a proud cat parent, indeed.

He continued to grow, become healthy and wound up with a long, thin body and long legs. He had pale sherbet orange fur and was marked with a barely visible ticking in a striped pattern along his back. All four paws had white socks, and he had tuxedo markings. He sported a white mustache and white fur that covered the underside of his chin and trailed down, covering his chest. His white-tipped tail was long with thick fur in an orange stripe pattern. All his fur was short, very thick and velvety. It was rewarding to pet Prince, and we pet him often.

Over the course of time, however, we nicknamed him Flippy-the-Fish, after observing his comical behavior of rolling over and over, flipping back and forth on his back with his feet and legs straight up in the air. Since his fur was orange like a goldfish, Flippy-the-Fish seemed like a more logical name for him than Prince. Although, the naming of the kitten did not stop there. Mr. Dandy Boots was also entirely fitting with his well-defined, white socks well up over his feet. He reminded me a little of "Puss in Boots" from the fairy tales by Charles Perrault. Fusty did not like the name, Mr. Dandy Boots. He acted fussy and indignant when we used this name. He responded positively, though, when we called him, Flippy-the-Fish. That was all we needed to say—Flippy-the-Fish, and he flipped onto his back, ready to go into action.

In the end, we settled on Fusty. Fusty was the name that came out of our mouths—the name we could remember to call him. This kitten had so many unique and fancy titles, we decided to keep them all and call him Fusty for short. Our new kitten had the longest name of any cat we knew: Prince, Flippy-the-Fish—Fusty, Mr. Dandy Boots. This must have been a lucky name, for this was the beginning of a new life for this lucky kitten. What a name! What a cat!

It took a little work, but over time he transformed from a traumatized, abandoned kitten into a healthy, vibrant, well-adjusted young cat out exploring his world! He felt safe and cared for now, and he became playful, like the kitten he still was. It was apparent that this young cat had reclaimed his kittenhood. Outdoors, he ran up the maple trees twitching his great, long tail excitedly. With his ears and tail straight up in the air, he raced across the lawns at top speed chasing imaginary rabbits or squirrels. His short fur became thick, velvety and luxurious. He was exquisite. His once dark, betrayed, heartbroken eyes now sparkled with joy, excitement and curiosity. It was gratifying to see him rehabilitate into such a confident young cat. It made my life feel very worthwhile.

It had not been a problem for me to adopt this kitten and take good care of him, as I had the great fortune to work out of an office trailer parked on the driveway of our property. I was my own boss and set my daily schedule. I had the advantage of working hours that made sense for taking time out to care for the kitten and managing the office. It just seemed to all fall into place. I never once worried about the time I was spending on office work or the time needed to care for Fusty. I believed synchronicity was all around and was there to support me in this venture because adopting this kitten was "meant to be," so to speak. Things flowed right into place for me when it came to taking care of the kitten. I felt fortunate. I had the time and the means. We were living the good life—that is for sure.

As TIME PASSED, FELLER and I wound up on the same page about Fusty needing life skills and survival training. It was plain to see, he did not know how to take care of himself. He knew nothing, nothing at all. Feller took him under his tutelage and began teaching him the basics of survival beyond the safety of the fence. Fusty was in training from then on, and the two cats were always together after that.

Feller taught Fusty how to catch mice and eat them, starting with the head first—*crunch, crunch, crunch.* During health exams, the veterinarian marveled at their clean, white teeth. It was crunching through bones, especially the skull that kept their teeth in perfect condition. Eating wild prey and healthy cat food kept Feller and Fusty in top form. They were never sick.

Feller was semi-feral and could survive almost any conditions the wild world out in the county had to offer. He possessed a balanced combination of caution and confidence. He paid good attention to Fusty and passed down all his knowledge to him. Day after day, the scene was Feller heading out through the slit cut into the wires of the fence with Fusty following right behind. It was so precious and unbelievable. It was a heartwarming experience to watch their relationship develop. Feller and Fusty became brothers.

One day I was confident that Fusty had made a full recovery when he came home dragging a full-grown rabbit he had killed. After he ate his fill of the quarry, he buried it in the front yard beneath a bush. He hid the rabbit by covering it with grass that he scratched up with his claws. He followed everything Feller taught him. That mid-summer day, Fusty graduated first in his survival skills class (he was the only one in his class, but that does not matter). Now, if for any reason he wound up left all alone or on his own, he would be able to survive. He earned an A+ on all accounts.

Feller and Fusty spent their summer days hunting and exploring the vast, vacant fields that stretched far beyond our property. They slept outdoors in our shed all summer long and lived off the rodents they caught and carried home between their teeth every day. They slept on cozy cat beds perched on the workbench in front of the window. All summer long, they came and left as they pleased. These were two adult male cats who were confident, natural cats.

During the freezing winter months, they spent their time

indoors with us. Feller slept upstairs with us on the bed, and Fusty slept in the dining room on the lowboy chair. These cats were living the dream, the good life. Everything a cat could want in this life was right here in their home in the county. We were all enjoying county life and knew it just did not get any better. By this time, we were a happy and contented family of four: Jerry, Leanna, Feller and Fusty.

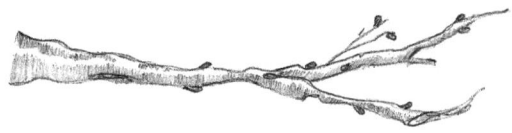

Chapter Two

Do Sasquatch Scream?

T HE YEARS AND THE seasons passed. We worked, we played, and we kept our small company afloat. Our lives were going splendidly well. Perhaps it was the peace and natural beauty surrounding our home that got started me on the most unexpected adventure of my life.

One day out of nowhere, I suddenly became interested in Sasquatch, and that was quite out of the ordinary for me. I had no idea why or where the sudden interest was coming from, but I felt an urgency to learn whatever I could about this legendary creature of the Pacific Northwest. So, I began my search for answers by looking for anything I could find online. Soon, I discovered there were Sasquatch books, blogs and lots of videos available right at my fingertips.

I began by reading several of what appeared to be first-hand experiences written by individuals who claimed to have encountered Sasquatch. Some of their stories seemed credible and really caught my attention. What made these stories, in particular, seem convincing was that each of them contained a common theme that described how a possible encounter with an unknown species might play out. Usually, the Sasquatch was helping a hiker or camper who was either injured or lost in the deep forest. A Sasquatch or number of Sasquatch came to their aid and rescued them. The stories typically ended with the Sasquatch safely escorting the lost individual out of the wilderness or to a sheltered landing point, where they could reach safety on their own. The information I was reading stayed within the realm of good, old-fashioned horse sense, the kind of sense "God gave a Billy Goat," as they used to say back in the olden days.

I also noted none of the realistic encounters described Sasquatch as dangerous, harmful beasts. I found that interesting. In some of the cases, though, the Sasquatch may have been irritated that a human being wound up in their territory with an emergency, but they took it upon themselves to rescue the injured or lost person. I concluded, if Sasquatch were ferocious and potentially dangerous beings, it would be common knowledge by now—their terror and danger would be well publicized. These are the stories that made sense and seemed like they could be actual, genuine encounters. They were not fantastical but were sound and grounded in common sense.

I was also gathering from these stories that Sasquatch are shy and elusive. For the most part, they did not want to be seen by human beings and were usually hiding or bolting out of the area where they were spotted. They sounded like a species of beings that could hide and be living in our isolated wilderness areas.

I watched several amateur videos of both Sasquatch and Big Foot. As I surveyed these two main categories, dozens of videos lined up for viewing. Obviously, many people either believe in the existence of Sasquatch or are unsure and, like me, searching for the truth.

I learned that Sasquatch has many other names: Big Foot, Yeti and Skunk Ape, to name just a few. In the Pacific Northwest, the name Sasquatch is a coastal Native American word that means "wild man." Each different Sasquatch name brought up a different variety of videos to choose from.

Some of these videos impressed me and seemed credible, as in the instance where a Sasquatch caught on film was shown leaving the area very quickly. This depiction of the Sasquatch fleeing the scene agreed with my basic understanding of the natural world. It remains true for me to this day that an elusive, rarely seen creature would do its best to stay hidden from sight. Therefore, if they did exist, they must be seriously elusive—otherwise, we would have abundant evidence of their existence on camera.

There was much to speculate upon. It seemed that much of what was known about Sasquatch required a leap of faith to believe in their existence, even with what concrete evidence we have at present. The 'faith' part, I believe, made it all so challenging. I think our culture prefers scientific evidence. I, too, was searching for something concrete, something believable beyond a doubt that Sasquatch are here with us. I had a lot of researching to do, and I had so many questions. Fortunately, there was lots of information out there for me to uncover.

I felt it would be remarkable if another species of being coexisted here along with us. Humanity has always appeared lonely to me. We need another species here with us. Right now, humans could use a friend and helping hand to learn how to live with nature rather than against it. I was searching for the existence of another species to fill in the gap between how human beings live versus living cooperatively with nature. I hoped Sasquatch existed. I truly hoped that there was something to this mysterious legend after all. I wanted Sasquatch to be real.

THERE WERE OTHER SITES and writings that were scientific in nature. This information provided me with some practical knowledge about footprints, hair specimens, and areas where Sasquatch are found. It gave me more foothold on the subject, and I learned there is abundant evidence of this kind. Numerous Sasquatch researchers focused on this type of scientific evidence to substantiate and document their findings. It was their basic premise of proof that Sasquatch exist.

I had been aware of stories and reports about personal encounters with Sasquatch during the young adult years of my life. Many years ago, I read a piece written by the late President Theodore Roosevelt, who in 1893 wrote in a memoir about encountering Big Foot on a wilderness hunting expedition. In his story, Big Foot was a large creature that stood upright on two legs. At one point in his writing, he remarked that the creature had trashed their expedition camp and left footprints behind that were humanlike and not like those of a bear.

Also, I knew a few people who claimed to have seen a Sasquatch, but I did not have the clarity nor the experience to consider the possibility of whether their stories were true. I had always kept an open mind, but these were their stories, and they never made any headway toward proof of the existence of Sasquatch. Nothing came of their stories. They simply remained stories... Half of me believed it was all a myth, but the other half of me had an inkling Sasquatch just may be a species here on Earth. I was driven to find the truth.

There have been sightings all around the world and especially in North America over the course of many years. With thousands of square miles designated as wilderness areas, it seemed possible that an unknown species could still be undiscovered by man. If

Sasquatch were intelligent creatures, it was likely they could be living deep in the wilderness undetected.

THEN ONE DAY, I came across some homemade internet videos with supposed audio vocalizations of Sasquatch labeled "Screaming Bigfoot and/or Sasquatch Screams." I decided to listen to some of these videos and wondered if, by chance, a more dangerous side of Sasquatch might be revealed—a terrifying, hairy, ape-like creature snarling with bared fangs and drool overflowing from its mouth. Perhaps there does exist a dangerous beast, dangerous to man? I was curious.

As I checked out several of the screaming Sasquatch videos, I could not identify any vocalizations that sounded like screaming. In my estimation, screaming and what I was hearing did not link up correctly. I looked up the dictionary definition for "scream" to clarify precisely what scream means. To scream is to vocalize long and loud. It is a way to express pain or a lot of emotion. I replayed the videos repeatedly, listening for some emotional quality based on this definition. Of the audio recordings that seemed potentially valid, I did not hear any vocalizations that would fit the definition of "scream." Although, I did hear howling. The howling intrigued me but was more like an expression of communication than anything else. I pushed on.

The howling sounded similar to wolves, communicating from one pack member to another. Most other animals living in the wild display the same behavior. They call out, long and loud, to locate other mammals of like kind. Birds chirp long and loud when trying to attract a mate before nesting in spring. In early fall, bull elk whistle long and loud during the rut or mating season.

The howling in these videos was loud and sounded like it came from a mammal—though it didn't sound like any warm-blooded animal I had ever heard before. I found that compelling.

I could not come up with any animal living in the United States that could make a sound quite like the howling on these particular recordings. As a matter of fact, the howling sounded more like the voice of a human—which really caught my attention.

The intensity of the vocalizations did cause me fear, as I had never heard a sound quite like that before. The magnitude of the vocalization was incredible. The creature howling must have been gigantic in size, as the lung capacity sounded much greater than ours. The creature that made this huge sound needed to be equally as huge.

Meanwhile, the mournful howling did, in fact, give me goosebumps as I listened, but not because it was scary. I must admit; it was alarming to hear a sound I could not identify and quite that loud, yet I could not tear myself away. I got a sense of the creature making these howling sounds. It sounded like a creature that very little is known about, an undiscovered creature of some kind. That was the sense I got as I listened. Too, these vocalizations did not sound like a hoax. My gut instinct told me these were real. Then it was time to turn away, to turn the howling off, and go on with the rest of the day.

FELLER AND FUSTY HAD quite the experience as they, too, were listening. The cats and I hung out together a lot, and they were both lying on the floor near my feet flicking their tails up and down against the carpet. I knew my cats well, and it was clear to me they were carefully studying the howling as if to pinpoint what animal was at hand. They were the apex predators on our property, were protective and kept the rodent population to a bare minimum. Feller and Fusty did not demonstrate fear but rather interest. I thought the cats were not startled because the howling sounded normal to them and perfectly in tune with the natural world.

Feller, Fusty and I wound up outside in the backyard, watching the wind blow the tops of the tall, popular trees. It was typical for the wind to begin blowing in the evening; it was growing chilly outside. The tree branches waved back and forth against the still vibrant blue sky. The sun was sinking below the horizon now. Seagulls soared high on the wind, slowly zigzagging their way home to roost. The evening was settling in, and all the animals, birds and insects were slowing down, ready to find a place to nestle in for the night.

The cats stretched out comfortably on the thick, mossy lawn while I reclined on the folding lounge chair. It was too early to start dinner, so we soaked up the peace and quiet in the yard together as we waited for Jerry to return home from work. It was the end of a good day.

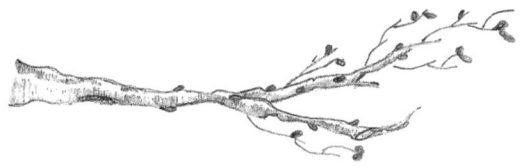

Chapter Three

High Strangeness

D URING MY RESEARCH, I came across some exciting writings and conference presentations by noteworthy Sasquatch experiencers. I noticed that the subject of paranormal interactions came up often for the experiencers and seemed to be a major part of their relationship with Sasquatch. According to these experiencers, the Sasquatch possesses supernatural powers that come naturally to them. When they meet and greet their human friends, these powers can occur in highly unexpected and unusual ways. This can be pretty surprising for human beings. Furthermore, during these conference presentations, experiencers affectionately referred to these interactions with Sasquatch as "strangeness" or "high strangeness."

I had no idea what was meant by these terms—until I began to have baffling experiences myself. Unexplainable oddball things started happening to me during the course of a typical day, but at that time, I did not connect these peculiar incidences with Sasquatch. It did not occur to me that these were actual encounters.

I will just say that it was a really confusing time, a head-scratcher, as it were.

My first paranormal experience began right after I twisted my left knee in early autumn of 2017. I damaged the meniscus to the point that walking became problematic. I could not straighten my left leg without excruciating pain. It is necessary to straighten our knees while we walk. It is that simple.

Since my new diagnosis of pre-diabetes, walking has been high on my list of priorities. Walking and diet change was my doctor's primary prescription. I had committed to myself that I would follow the doctor's orders on this one. My health was important to me.

In search of a solution to answer the problem that my left knee was creating, I began studying information that compared the leg movement differences between apes and humans. Apes do not need to straighten their knees while they walk. They keep them in a bent position. I found several comparisons with pictures and diagrams focused on knee movements and studied them carefully. Essentially, when apes walk, their knees remain in a bent position. Not only do human beings both bend and straighten their knees, they also lock them as they walk.

I continued searching for some way to get the necessary walks I badly needed. After all, it could take my knee six months to a year to heal, and I worried that by then, the muscles in both my knee and leg would have atrophied. Maybe it could be possible to walk without straightening my knee? Could I walk with my knee ever so slightly bent? I was ready to give it a try and hoped that keeping my knee bent would be a temporary solution. I just needed my knee to heal.

I came across an interesting article that compared the walking movements of Sasquatch to that of Homo Sapiens. This was an unexpected find. In this study, the report suggested that Sasquatch exists and is *Gigantopithecus blacki,* an extinct ape that stood approximately nine feet tall. This ape lived in southern China during the Pleistocene Epoch. The article further stated *Gigantopithecus* habituate the wilderness areas of the world—and though rarely seen, they are mistaken for Sasquatch. This was interesting.

After reading the material about *Gigantopithecus,* I was convinced for several weeks that Sasquatch were living in our wilderness areas. I further surmised that all the Sasquatch sightings in the world were *Gigantopithecus.*

Satisfied that I had found the answer as to whether Sasquatch was real, I stopped my research and debate over the whole Sasquatch issue. With my knee giving me some real grief, I was not sure I was up to the challenge of uncovering the truth about their existence. It was much simpler and reassuring to stumble across this more logical, scientific answer. So, not needing any more details on the subject, I closed the chapter on the Sasquatch investigation for now.

However, I continued studying the article to find a way to exercise without further injury to my knee. I read that for the giant prehistoric apes to keep their balance while walking upright, their arms needed to sway from front to back. Interestingly, this arm-swinging directly correlated to a video I watched during my initial research on Sasquatch, the famous Patterson-Gimlin footage taken in October of 1967 at Bluff Creek in Northern California. A Bigfoot was filmed walking away from a startled cameraman on horseback. In the film, the Bigfoot swung its arms front to back while quickly walking out of sight and into the woods.

I DECIDED TO SET aside time each day to practice walking while keeping my sore knee slightly bent. I spent two to three weeks practicing, and after a while, I was getting the hang of it. Even though it was unnatural for me to walk this way, I kept it up. I practiced walking back and forth across the lawn. It took a lot of energy, but my knee was not bothered by these efforts. This was encouraging.

One afternoon, an opportunity arose for me to put the walking technique to the test and, at the same time, get in some badly needed exercise. I was parked downtown and decided the flat sidewalks would be the perfect testing grounds. Carefully, I stepped forward slowly with my knee slightly bent and found I could walk without pain. I was delighted!

I walked a fair distance through town along the sidewalks enjoying the sense of freedom. After a while, I decided I had better not overdo it and turned back toward my parked car to head home. At that very moment, a crippling pain began radiating up from my knee. Next, a hammering fatigue pounded against every inch of my body. I stopped dead in my tracks.

Barely able to take another step, I panicked. I did not know how I would make it back to my car. I urgently needed to get the weight off my left knee. I needed help—severe pain was shooting out from my knee and up my leg. I wished Jerry were here to handle everything and get me home. Unfortunately, I left my cell phone at home, of course! I had never felt so stuck in my life.

The next thing I knew, I began to feel strange support from somewhere—physical and emotional support. It was as if someone was on both my right and left sides, helping me walk. The next thing I knew, I was able to walk with no pain. In fact, at that moment, walking became easy.

Curiously, my panic disappeared as I continued toward my car. Puzzling and strange as this was, I enjoyed the support, though I was bewildered. In my mind, I kept asking, "Where is this coming from? What is this?" I glanced up and looked around at the other people in the crosswalk with me, and they did not seem to notice anything unusual.

Then the answer came to me abruptly. A picture of two sets of thin legs flashed powerfully into my brain. I could see fleshy legs covered with long, soft auburn hair from the knees down to the ankles walking alongside me. I could not see any feet but could see that the legs were there. But they were not there. I could not explain it to myself—real, flesh-and-blood legs were walking alongside me. I could feel them there; I could see them there. It felt like two individuals were helping me walk. I wondered about holograms—are they real, and could I be seeing one?

The support was powerful. Each time I looked down toward the pavement, I could see the legs. Soon, I saw my car, and suddenly the legs and the support disappeared. Instantly, the pain returned to my knee. I was exhausted and confused. Fortunately, I was only a few steps from my car.

AFTER I GOT HOME, I took Ibuprofen, elevated my sore knee and rested on the couch. After a while, my knee felt better, so I got up and called out for the cats. Feller and Fusty came running in from the hay fields—Feller leading the way. Fusty followed close behind, batting at Feller's tail as if to say, "Hurry up. I'm the boss here!" I petted and talked to them. With their tails straight up, they rubbed back and forth across my ankles, purring loudly. These were the best cats ever.

It was late summer, yet the sun hung high for hours. I sat out on the patio under the shade of the surrounding sunflowers, watching the sky peek between their tall, flowering heads. The sunflower patio is where I sat when I needed rebalancing and restoring—this is where my reset button gets pushed. I stayed out on the patio until Jerry got home from work.

I watched him back in and park in front of the office with his white work van.

Jerry grabbed a beer and joined the cats and me. Later, I

prepared a simple dinner of scrambled eggs and toast, as I needed to take it easy on that knee. Together we shared our stories of the day. When it came time for me to share, I left out my experience in town. I was not comfortable telling anyone what had happened. I did not know what to think about it myself. I was left wondering what had taken place that day in town. Needing plenty of time to process my strange experience, I tried to put it out of my mind for the time being. I simply could not think about it. I had no possible way to understand what did or did not happen. It was too confusing.

LATER THAT EVENING, WE all snuggled in for the night. Our routine was set in stone, and we followed it faithfully. Tomorrow would come, and there would be a whole new set of adventures. I always looked forward to my first cup of tea each morning.

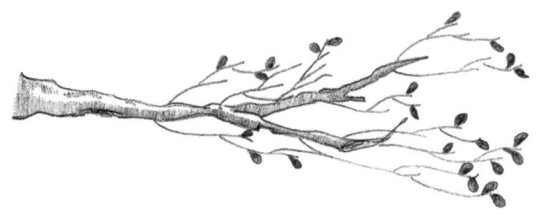

Chapter Four

Office Trailer Pranks

O UR BUSINESS OFFICE WAS a trailer that we remodeled using leftover building materials from past jobs we had completed. We kept the office trailer permanently parked on our driveway. The office was beautiful with a nice paint job, carpet, an overhead skylight and sliding windows that were unused and left over from a drive-up coffee stand that never got built. This is where I did all the bookkeeping and where Jerry worked with building drawings, bids, contracts and invoices at the plan table. Our office location at home on the driveway was one of the perks we enjoyed as self-employed people.

At 9:00 AM each morning, work began, and I had only to walk out to the driveway to reach the office. Once inside, there were great views of the countryside from the window at the desk. My big excitement for the day was heading to the nearest Starbucks for my tall, soy, no-water chai tea latte. Any time I wanted a break, I took off. I had only myself to answer to. Yes! I loved my work life!

One morning while sitting down at my desk, I noticed bright sunlight glinting sharply off the rooftop of an old, abandoned farm building out beyond a stand of fir trees across a field. It stood lonely and uncared for. A short ways further out was a sorry, neglected chicken coop. The two old buildings sagged heavily at their midsections, the weight of their roofs dragging them down to the ground and imploding inward upon themselves. I could see piles of cedar shake shingles scattered all over the ground. "Now, there's some good kindling," I uttered. Jerry had built a brick fire pit in the backyard. We loved building campfires and the feel of being outdoors.

I opened the mail and afterward coded the payroll time sheets for the crew. Later while paying bills, I heard what sounded like driveway gravel bouncing off the roof. I looked up toward the ceiling and through the skylight to see only the gigantic branches of the cedar tree sweeping down like a great broom above the roof. Yellow rays of sunlight poured into the office. It was a beautiful morning.

I paid no attention. There was nothing there to see, so I went back to work. *Plunkity, plunk, thunk*—again, something bounced off the roof. "What could that be—a bird?" I wondered if a heavy bird like a crow or maybe a raven was hopping across the top of the trailer. "A bird walking over the roof would make a sound like that," I told myself.

I decided to investigate as an excuse to go outside for a moment to breathe fresh air, something I loved to do often. I stepped out into the bright morning sunshine and took it all in. While outside, I took a few breaths of air and mildly checked for any potential source that might explain the noise. I could not see anything, so I figured the roof was cracking naturally, the wood expanding and contracting from cool and damp back to warm and dry. Honestly, I had never heard it crack quite like that before.

I returned to my work and settled back in again at my desk. A few moments after I started to work, louder thwacking sounds broke the silence. They were noisy and had increased in frequency, making a constant barrage, rapping against the tar roof shingles, Thunkity-Thunk-Thunk. It was slightly comical. I lost interest because it did not make sense in my world; therefore, it was something to ignore. I was busy with a long list of tasks to finish. I didn't give it any more thought. I had my work to do.

THAT EVENING FOR DINNER, I made one of our favorite comfort foods: ham, cheese and lima bean casserole. As we quietly ate our meal together, I mentioned to Jerry that the trailer roof was making a lot of cracking noises. He did not give it much thought and kept eating.

The next morning the temperature dropped. Our routine changed as we adjusted to the beginnings of colder weather. Winters were mighty cold in this area. Freezing temperatures typically lasted throughout the winter and did not slacken until spring.

Now, autumn was settling in. Mist and gray clouds darkened the sky, and the days grew shorter. The chilly air was wet with moisture. Jerry and I watched the news together in the evenings, as it was becoming too cool to sit outside on the garden patio. The patio sunflowers were getting regular visits now from chickadees that picked off the nutritious seeds from the large, bent-over flower heads. Squirrels discovered the sunflowers and climbed their broad stalks clutching mightily to the seed-packed flower heads, and all the while, they made a big mess of seeds all over the ground.

The warmly furred cats remained outside, still insisting on hunting, their favorite activity. They were not ready to commit to the warmth of the house just yet. Usually, they would continue to sleep outside until the freezing northeasters began blasting their way through the county. It was usually at this point the temperature and wind chill let them know it was time to come indoors.

The next morning was chilly as I headed out for work. While I started planning the errands for the day, the rock pelting started again right away—but this time, the rapping, tapping and plunking was more like an assault across the rooftop, *Wappity-Wap-Wap*. It was impressive! It reminded me of a snowball fight, only with gravel rather than snowballs. I chuckled and stepped outside to investigate but saw nothing unusual. I did not expect to see anything, so I gave up and went back to my desk.

Consistent with the attacks the day before, the noisy missiles started again just as I sat back down. Quickly, I ran back out the door once more to look, if only to make sure whether this was my imagination or not. Predictably, the noises stopped once I was out on the porch. It was quite something. I had never encountered anything quite like it before, and the roof had sounded like it was getting a thorough walloping. I made a few failed attempts to make sense of what was going on. The incident seemed rather suspicious.

Then I remembered reading stories back during the beginning phases of my Sasquatch research about people who lived near Sasquatch. In several stories, the Sasquatch tended to throw things like pinecones toward their human neighbors. It was done out of consideration for the humans and was a gentle way of letting the humans know the Sasquatch were nearby.

I also read that Sasquatch children were allowed to play around humans, whom the Sasquatch parents felt were safe. Some of the Sasquatch children enjoyed playing harmless pranks on unsuspecting humans. In some cases, the humans became agitated, and the Sasquatch adults courteously intervened and stopped the jokes and antics. Just as in the case of human parents, Sasquatch parents understand how rambunctious children can be. Thinking back, I remember playing pranks on my unsuspecting siblings and friends as a child. This was beginning to sound familiar and very ordinary to me.

For the rest of the week, I listened while the roof came under attack. I came to expect it. It made me chuckle, and I finally burst out laughing, laughing at the goofiness of it. "What is this? Could this really be Sasquatch children?" I laughed and enjoyed the possibility this might be a good joke.

SUDDENLY, I REMEMBERED THE joke I loved playing on Jerry while he worked away in the office trailer. Sometimes when the mood struck me, I stepped out into the backyard and hurled a piece of driveway gravel over the 6-foot fence and onto the trailer roof to get Jerry's attention, especially if it was dinner time. I aimed directly for the plexiglass skylight right smack in the middle of the convex top, wanting to make a loud and impressive *Thwack-o* to get his attention.

Once I had accomplished making a loud and irritating noise directly over his head, I quickly ran back into the house, laughing and feeling very clever. I tried to make it back inside before Jerry bolted out of the office, glancing swiftly from side to side—but he was fast, and I was rarely fast enough. Usually, he would hear the screen door slamming shut behind me. Quickly, figuring out that not only was a prank being played on him but that it was *me* doing the pranking, he would come inside for dinner, and we both would have a good laugh. We were in love and had lots of fun.

ONE FRIDAY AFTERNOON, JERRY spent some time in the office working over building drawings for a remodel job. I was preparing to do the payroll. In the construction industry, the crew got paid every Friday. To my surprise, the roof pelting started while we were both working. I did not expect this to happen with Jerry in the office. I had thought this was a joke explicitly intended for me, a payback for all the times I played jokes and pranks on others, especially Jerry. However, the onslaught of *rapping and thwapping* noises was as spectacular a performance as could be imagined. It was so stunning that Jerry stepped outside, just as I had done. The show stopped abruptly as he searched around from underneath the porch overhang. He glanced around  once more and returned to his calculations at the plan table.

Just as Jerry got back to work, the assault picked right back up where it left off full throttle directly overhead, *Thwackity-Thwack-Thwack-o!* "Well, I'll be," he said. "I wonder what is making that sound." However, Jerry quit noticing and worked through the ambush of the driveway gravel and gave it no more thought. He was the type of person that accepted all sounds as a part of life and never allowed strange or unusual sounds to bother him. He was very mellow this way. I admired this characteristic a great deal and only wished I was just like him, sigh.

I was pleased that Jerry witnessed some of the roof noises I had been talking about during our dinners together. Shortly after that, the pummeling stopped altogether and never started up again. I missed the barrage of invisible, silly missiles and was sad when it ended. Later that fall, when the gutters were cleaned, we did not find any extra displaced driveway gravel on the roof. It remains a mystery to this day what those noises on the office trailer roof were all about. Mysteries are so much fun. What would we do without them?

Chapter Five

Cats Like to Play
More High Strangeness

S HORTER DAYS CLOSED IN fast this year, turning out any light in the sky by early evening. The temperatures dropped down into the thirties, and pouring rain soaked the land causing rivers to flood. Fir trees with water-logged branches bent over, helplessly reaching for the ground. Strong wind gusts wailed through the county, snapping tree limbs and knocking out power lines. Winter was on its way.

Morning was cold and dark when Jerry left for work, and it was cold and dark when he returned at the end of the day. I was especially grateful this time of year that our office trailer was parked close to the house. For me, it made getting to work a piece of cake.

I began making homemade soups during cold weather. One

favorite was chicken and corn chowder. I used local sweet corn that I had blanched and frozen during the warm summer months, summer months that seemed so long ago and sadly forgotten. We lived on the soups, one after another, during the long, cold winters.

The cats stayed inside the house most of the time now and sat near my feet with their tails curled around their bodies, just hanging out. Some evenings when they were a little bored, they began wrestling. Feller, the dominant cat, knew how to take wrestling advantages and began by flipping over on his back, right up

against Fusty with all four paws pointed upwards on the offensive.

Swiftly, Feller swatted at Fusty, who either sat or stood over him, swatting back with carefully chosen chopstick-style motions. He was a Prince, after all—he seemed to be wondering why this wild rabble messed with him in the first place. He kept his ears pointed slightly back in both playful puzzlement and irritation. Fusty did not understand Feller, but he loved him and put up with his irritating antics.

Feller's velvety, black and gray blotched fur appeared menacing, like a throwback coloration from an ancient species. He was beautiful with stunning markings. Fusty was not thwarted in the least, just mildly irritated.

Finally, Fusty had enough and chased Feller back and forth across the floor. Feller was delighted! As they scampered, their feet thumped heavily in the chase. In the dining room, where the floor was slick, we watched as they comically ran in place at top speed, scrambling in earnest to get traction to peel out ahead of one another. Their extended claws scratched uselessly over the smooth wooden surface. A spectacular show; it was entertainment at its finest.

They chased one another across the kitchen and into the living room for what seemed like hours. After a while, they grew tired of the game and curled up together on the carpet to sleep. Now every evening, the four of us just hung out together. Meanwhile, night crept in quietly with an air of darkness and solitude. We all lay low as if dormant, each of us listening to the stillness, secretly waiting for spring to arrive.

AFTER THE QUIET AND uneventful evening, we went to bed early. I felt more tired than usual with the darkness closing in around us so early. I dragged myself to the bedroom, and Feller followed—he slept on top of Jerry, of all things. Fusty was curled up on the low-boy chair downstairs in the corner of the dining room. His eyes were already closed for the night, even before the rest of us were heading to bed.

I settled down quickly and began dozing off right away. The silence was restful, and the peace instantly took me to a place where I could forget the never-ending grind of the company. Owning a company came with lots of responsibility and liability; this was something we never escaped and was certainly not one of the perks of owning our own business. The pressure from the responsibility went on endlessly day after day.

My rest became interrupted when I woke up and saw movements out of the corner of my eye—odd black shadows were moving around in the room. The shadows were not just black—they were blacker than black. In the darkness, I could see forms moving like clouds or maybe smoke moving around as if in a gentle breeze. Sometimes hazy and sometimes speckled and viscous, the black shadows moved around the bedroom in the dark. They seemed energized like your skin would tingle if you touched one.

I was pretty alarmed, and although the shadows did not feel dangerous, they made me nervous just the same. I had no idea what I was seeing. The blackness of the shadows was impenetrable and seemed alive.

Alert with eyes wide open, I could not fall back to sleep. I pointed out the shadows to Jerry, but he said he could not see anything. I continued to watch the shadows. I wished I was in a dream and would wake up with everything back to normal. At some point during the night, I succumbed to sleep.

In the morning, I was concerned about the shadows in the bedroom and wondered what they could be? I was timid about anything out of the ordinary and outside of my usual sphere of reality.

The black shadows appeared at bedtime every night over that entire winter. It was nerve-racking. There were many nights I could not take it and left for the spare bedroom to feel safer. I kept my eyes closed, so whether the shadows followed me to the spare room, I never knew. I thought I had no other defense but to remove myself and block my vision. I needed to feel safe in order to fall asleep. No matter how I felt about the shadows, they appeared every night. Jerry could not see them.

I tried to deny that anything different or strange was happening, and our work schedule continued with the usual grind. In the office, I recalled the thin, hairy legs that had helped me walk near the end of that summer. I wondered if the shadows I was seeing were coming from the same source as the thin, hairy legs. I had been avoiding the idea, but finally, I considered whether this might be Sasquatch.

But how could this be Sasquatch? My impression of Sasquatch was nothing like the black, inky shadows on the bedroom walls. I was bewildered and confused, with no hope for any answers. These experiences were not matching up with any of the stories I had read during my research about Sasquatch.

Over a period of a few weeks, different details about the shadows slowly became more apparent. At times they took on a form of some kind. Usually, I sealed my eyes shut when this occurred. Often, during the day and at night, I could feel the presence of another being around me, and at times I felt like I was being watched. It was an odd feeling. It was not scary; I just felt watched. My gut sense was that someone was trying to make contact with me. I mentioned to Jerry a few more times that I was still seeing the shadows. Several times, we turned out the lights while I pointed and explained where and what to look for. But he could not see the shadows, and I could not understand how that was possible. They were obvious to me. I felt very alone and did not know where to turn for help or an explanation.

One day I asked Jerry if he thought maybe I was seeing things that are not there. He answered, "Leanna, you are seeing what you are seeing. It's okay." Jerry had no idea what was happening when I asked for his opinion or help. He was completely stumped. He did not want me to be nervous or frightened, but he had no answers except to reassure me in his own way. So, I stopped asking him about the shadows. I could see them; he could not. I worked hard to make this okay.

I felt lost with no one to turn to or talk with about what was happening. Only because of Jerry did I feel safe; thank goodness for him and his calm, steady demeanor. His inability to see the shadows gave me hope that one day I would no longer see them myself. I took this hope to bed with me each and every night.

As the months began nearing the end of winter and the cold air slowly began to get warm, I had a feeling that something was being asked of me. I sensed a group of human-like beings that wanted to meet me and connect with me. Mentally, though, I kept pushing the idea as far away from me as possible. I was not open to contact of any kind from anything out of the norm. The strangeness of the situation was overpowering, yet I felt safe. Somehow, I had the wherewithal to hang in there because I knew nothing wrong or dangerous would happen. I would remain safe and secure, even though I could not piece together the puzzling events that were going on.

OVER TIME, I ACCEPTED that maybe we were not the only species of humans living and breathing here on Earth. Humanity was struggling with several serious issues worldwide. Science kept us very aware by reporting that everything was headed in the wrong direction in terms of climate change. The news became a source of stress. There was no hope for a viable solution toward a better climate here on Earth. To add to the chaos, there were world leaders who struggled to maintain power and sovereignty. Other nations even threatened to "push the nuclear weapons button" and start a war. We were faced with massive declining conditions right here on Earth every day.

Consequently, citizens worldwide were waiting for their governments to shift gears and change focus from the monotonous and ongoing world conflicts/chaos and begin taking significant, positive steps towards preserving Earth and preserving life, if you will. We were not facing the reality that we were busily erasing a future for ourselves here on our home planet. I often wondered if we needed an intervention to wake us up from all the distractions and face what we deny the most, change. Things need to change. In fact, nearly everything needed to change but especially our over-heating planet.

We need a change in many forms. But where do we start? Some problems need resolving, including the complicated layers of pollution in our world, the tyranny and threats of foreign invasion by powerful enemies, and a climate that has become hostile and dangerous. Was there anyone looking out for us? If so, please help us now before it is too late? These issues hung like a dark, heavy cloud covering the Earth. No continent, no country and no one was exempt from what was going on in our precious world. The end seemed imminent for everyone and our world.

Nevertheless, due to the strangeness of my situation and out of raw fear, I responded to the strange shadows on the wall with denial. I behaved as though nothing unusual was going on. Denial had never been my mode of operating before—but it was now. Mind-numbing denial felt like a reasonable recourse for mental safety and well-being. I was confused, and I wanted the shadows to go away. I tried to find the reset button in my life and push it in the hopes my chaotic but simple life would return to me. Maybe denying the odd things that were happening would make this all disappear. I hoped so.

Yet early every evening, shadows were there, moving across the walls. Then one day, there was a noticeable change in the shadows; they began to feel like a family—a legitimate, friendly family. A mother, father and children seemed to be anticipating meeting me. Next, I could feel love emanating from the shadows. Things were progressing in unpredictable ways. Of course, my fearful thinking expected disasters, but that was not what was unfolding... At first, the changes were foreign, but after a while, they felt more comfortable and safer. I was intrigued and continued to wonder if I was dealing with higher spiritual beings of some kind. Nonetheless, my internal conviction dictated that experiencing anything paranormal was still out of the question—although, by now, it seemed a little too late. It was already happening.

Once again, I ramped up my search about Sasquatch for more explicit personal information from experienced individuals involving Sasquatch encounters. Fortunately, I found several more conferences on the subject that were available on the Internet. Many of the presenters spoke freely about their personal experiences and interactions with what they believed to be Sasquatch.

The conferences were interesting, and I noticed a few similarities between the speakers. Some Sasquatch experiencers second-guessed themselves when something out of the ordinary occurred, something paranormal. "Did I hear a stomach growl? Was that me?" You know you heard the sound of a stomach growling, even though no one else was there with you. Still, common sense prevails and squashes the mere suggestion of invisible people out there who may have been hungry with an empty stomach. To my knowledge, it has not been an accepted idea that invisible people exist. Usually, the experiencers knew in that first instant that it was not their stomach and was someone else's. However, doubt sets in quickly, and they ask themselves if they really heard this sound.

I wanted to know if I was dealing with Sasquatch because my daily life had become unrecognizable. I yearned for things to smooth back out the way they were before… Let me tell you, that was one heck of a strange winter.

Chapter Six

Wow, Sasquatch! Hello!

S PRING LET OUT HER warm, gentle breath over the frozen landscape. Temperatures began rising into the high 40s and lower 50s. Tiny buds poked their green heads up along warming branches, and the sun peeked out slowly from between wildly unstable clouds, clouds that did not know whether to clear away in favor of blue sky or grow menacing and threaten thunder and lightning storms. Long awaited spring has sprung!

Once again, Feller and Fusty began sleeping outdoors in the shed. I kept their cozy cat beds on the worktable next to a window that looked out over the vegetable gardens. From the kitchen window, I could see them in their beds each morning as they began to awaken. I watched their long stretches and wide, gaping yawns exposing sharp, white teeth. I missed them when they lived outdoors. They really did seem to prefer it.

Spring was an exciting time, as the days were growing longer.

Now, when Jerry left for work, it was light outside, and it was still light upon his return home. We both had more energy during the longer, warmer days. I planned my garden boxes and began ordering seeds with great anticipation.

Our company got busier. Business owners who waited out the cold weather began requesting bids for tenant improvements one after another. New projects were coming along, and things started moving quickly. Jerry was busier somehow, even though he kept his crew going rain or shine all year long. Jobs filled the work schedule and were lined up several months out ahead. Jerry always managed to keep the company going full-time year-round, not an easy feat for a small, mom-and-pop-sized construction company.

THINGS WERE MOVING NICELY. Then one day, I felt someone watching me early one morning. While I was getting coffee at the kitchen window, I had a strange sensation that something was about to happen. I turned around, looking behind my back. I could feel a quickening in the air and felt sure that some strange and powerful force was around me. I took it for granted my creepy feelings were related to the shadowy figures in the bedroom that had shown up every night over the past several months. I kept noticing flashes and movements out of the corner of my eye. I jerked my head around often, trying to pinpoint the flashes of light and shadows. I sensed someone was behind me, following me. I kept looking over my shoulder, but no one would be there. It felt as though someone wanted my attention as if I was being summoned by an unknown force.

By the end of the day, late that March evening, it happened. The strange sensations I had been experiencing, the sense of being summoned, the moving shadows, the two thin, hairy legs and the invisible rocks pelting the trailer roof all clumped into a single moment of reckoning. As I stood in front of the large kitchen window, a powerful and intrusive message flashed like a lightning bolt into my brain, telling me to look up. Instantly, my head and eyes snapped up. As the bright light from inside the kitchen spilled out over the patio, I saw a hair-covered man standing nine feet away next to the barbecue. He was looking straight at me.

I froze, dumbstruck. I could not move. I was grateful I could breathe. I stood there frozen and just watched. Immediately, I noticed some details about the man. Not only was his body covered with hair, but his face was covered too. He was covered with soft, dark brown hair about four inches long. Around the face area, the hair was noticeably shorter, approximately two inches or less. Also, I could clearly see he was covered with hair, not fur.

I was surprised at how human he appeared. If this was Sasquatch, he was not scary or frightening, although he appeared massive. Without moving a muscle, I focused on his eyes; they were large and confident. To my astonishment, I could see each individual eyelash sprouting from his eyelids. This male being was a handsome individual by any set of standards. He seemed powerful and excessively sure of himself in a profound way. He possessed an inner strength that I had never before witnessed in any human being. I could see an unshakable confidence in his eyes. It was as though he had never experienced a weak moment or a negative thought in his entire life. It was unnerving, yet he was sublime. I was astonished.

He stood with his head slightly tilted down and over to one side in a peaceful gesture. He seemed pleased, like he had been anticipating this day for a long time, this moment when we would meet face to face. His arms were down at his sides, but I could not see his hands and could not move my eyes to look for them. I wondered if his arms were longer than the arms of humans as per the descriptions I had read about Sasquatch during my research.

I was frozen by an alien force of energy emanating from him. I literally could not move because of his intense energy. It made me anxious. I could not move.

I could observe the shape of the man's head and saw it was slightly conical. I could not make out whether he had a neck. All of his facial features were regular, like all human males. It was very evident that he was indeed human and unquestionably not an animal. He was human, but it was also just as clear that he was a *different* species of human. His appearance was just like ours except for his larger size, slightly conical-shaped head, hair covering, and so forth. It was possible he may have had longer arms than a human's, but I could not see if that was the case. I was frozen and could only see the upper part of him that was exposed within the confines of the window frame. He did not appear very different from us. His confidence was all-knowing in a benevolent, powerful way. Even though the situation was extraordinary and foreign, I knew I was witnessing someone significant and important. I was standing in front of someone great. I felt tiny in comparison, like an inferior, powerless being.

I remained frozen. I literally could not move. I could see what was going on but was under duress from the extraordinary energy radiating from him. It was straining my body to be that close to him. It reminded me of how my body felt when I dove to the bottom of the pool at the deep end during YMCA swimming classes while retrieving the rubber rings tossed out for me, the immense pressure from the weight of all that water bearing down on my body. It was similar but not similar. Similar only in that it was physical. It was not identical in that the force from the man-being felt different, unrecognizable. Possibly, he was a being with supernatural or magical energy not of this world. He seemed like magic. That was my best guess.

The encounter lasted too long, even though it had been only

a few moments. I could barely take the energy any longer and feared I would snap, although I did not know just how that would translate. I felt a great strain from the power of this man. I had never felt energy like it before. Then, an irresistible urge to fall asleep tried to overtake me; I could barely fight it off. I could feel the urge to sleep was directly due to the force of his energy.

To make things more complicated, I was going into shock. Every cell in my body was fighting to stay intact from the immense pressure pouring out from this being. Frozen and unable to move, I started heading toward a breaking point. It felt like every atom in my body was going to explode, shoot upward into the night sky and begin orbiting the Earth like space debris. And then, just as suddenly as he appeared, he disappeared. *Poof*—just like that, he was gone! He, who had been standing right on our concrete patio, vanished and left not a single trace that he had been standing right there in front of the window!

Quickly, I glanced over at my husband sitting at the dining room table just six feet away. He did not appear to have seen a thing. I was relieved on both counts: one, it was over, and two, Jerry had not seen this being. I had no plan to tell anyone what had just taken place. Stunned and unable to think, I went to bed.

The following morning was the beginning of a major life change for me. In the aftermath, I was exhilarated at first. Maybe I had seen a real Sasquatch! *Was* that a Sasquatch? He did not look like any images I had scoured over earlier in books and on the Internet. This individual did not look like an ape; he did not have long, sharp teeth like a fierce wild animal. Instead, he had a gentle and serene demeanor. I was not sure what I had just seen? It was becoming apparent that even though I had read everything I could find about this subject, I knew very little about Sasquatch and what they looked like. I had to guess this was Sasquatch. What else could it be?

VERY SOON AFTER, I unexpectedly became depressed. I was thrust into a process called "cognitive dissonance." Cognitive dissonance is a conflict between what is real and what is not. It can happen if we see something that does not exist. Cognitive dissonance can be uncomfortable. I was very uncomfortable, to say the least. My mind was overwhelmingly filled with conflict and subsequently ached. It ached in a way I had never experienced before. To process the sighting of something that does not exist and that only a relatively small number of people have witnessed was both overwhelming and mind-numbing. I remained depressed for several months, maybe a year. Cognitive dissonance takes time to get over.

Shortly after the cognitive dissonance set in, a second and equally disturbing reality began rearing its ugly head. It begged the question, "Maybe we are not alone on this planet in the way we think we are? For that matter, maybe we are not the dominant species either…"

After my experience seeing the powerful, hair-covered being, I could not return to my usual understanding of the world. What had been familiar, understandable and constant in my life was now obliterated, destroyed, wiped out. I was afraid and felt very alone. A backwash of stress filled every space inside my body and kept me panicky.

My worldview turned upside-down. There was no going back, not after what I saw. The idea we might not be the dominant species was terrifying. I was afraid to go outside for fear of seeing another powerful being or them seeing me. Maybe I was no longer safe outdoors?

After witnessing the Sasquatch on the patio, I could not look out my kitchen window for a long, long time. I passed right by while making dinner or washing dishes every day and every evening, making sure not to look through the glass into the darkness beyond. Furthermore, it slowly dawned on me that no one would believe my story. Oddly, I did not believe my story. I could not believe it because it was too surreal. Yet, I saw a hair-covered man, who was anxious to meet me, and who vanished. I saw this; I know I did. There was no denying it.

My head continued to ache. I was embroiled in too much mental conflict for my own good. One big question I asked myself over and over was, "Why did I see this hair-covered man, and who or what was he?" —An answer was not forthcoming. "I was all alone—or was I?"

A FEW WEEKS LATER, I decided it was time to tell Jerry about my encounter. He listened carefully, as he always did. He was patient and understanding, although he did not believe Sasquatch existed. He made his position clear that I had a right to have my own beliefs, and he had his. Sasquatch would never be one of his beliefs and that was okay. It had to be okay. Jerry stayed patient and supportive of me and what I was experiencing. He never judged me. We were always in support of each other.

However, I experienced very different responses from others when I finally did reach out to tell my story after a few months had passed. I decided to experiment to see what reactions I would get from a few friends, a couple of family members and a stranger at a party. Mostly, I got genuine interest and supportive responses; however, after a few minutes, irritation and no interest of any kind usually followed. Other times, the feedback was anger and even offense. I was stunned when one person turned away and walked off in a huff without saying a word. As I should have expected, there was a mixture of responses. Of course, I was most pleased by the friends and acquaintances who believed me. For some, it was too incredible a story to consider. I came to realize that this was too much to share with anybody.

After these few tries, I was convinced keeping my mouth shut was best for now. I decided no one needed to know. Keeping the experience to myself was safest. It also felt like I was protecting others by not exposing them to this story. To tell an account about an alien-type being living among us with an expectation to be believed is asking too much from others, no matter how sincerely or credibly you relay the tale. That is what I learned. I came to believe only people who have seen a Sasquatch or have other sub-stantial proof like vocalizations, footprints or pinecones thrown their way can believe they exist.

Sharing my story was too frightening for my family and friends. I needed to be sensitive about how unsettling this infor-mation might be for others hearing it for the first time. It had been terrifying for me at the beginning, back when I was get-ting my first signs of Sasquatch presence—I needed to remember that. What I went through was a progression, if you will. It was a sequence of strange occurrences. It did not take place all at once. To break out the whole picture to others may very well be over the top, too much for anybody to handle. So, I remained silent. It was pointless to tell my story. Besides, I had an awful lot to process myself, and I could see that it would take me some time, too!

One afternoon, while the skies were clear and sunny, I felt comfortable asking Jerry to join me outside on the patio and help solve a simple math equation. Carefully, I posed the ques-tion, "How tall do you think this visitor/being may have been?" I raised my arms over and above the barbecue to give Jerry an idea of how far up in feet and inches his head cleared over the top. Next, I pointed to where the visitor's head was facing at the window.

My general contractor husband, who earned a living by walk-ing through jobs with customers working out remodel details while simultaneously adding dimension measurements and figures in his head, quickly calculated and answered me, "Approximately eight feet tall." I admired his abilities. He was, without a doubt, my hero.

"Okay," I said. "Okay, that sounds about right. Thank you." That was the end of that. I made sure of it. I would not bring up the conversation of Sasquatch around my husband out of respect for his boundaries. We did not push our personal beliefs onto one another.

I soon discovered more websites containing conferences, meetings and speeches with respected Sasquatch experts and experiencers, some of whom had ongoing contact with Sasquatch. After my firsthand encounter at the kitchen window, I could compare my contact notes with their stories and descriptions. I had my own story now and was anxious to know how my experiences compared with others. I hoped to learn that my experiences fell within the norm.

Not all Sasquatch experiencers see a Sasquatch materialize—or dematerialize, for that matter. However, they often see other evidence that is more compelling, if not extraordinary. They find large, bare footprints in snow and/or mud, see evidence of trees ripped out of the ground or snapped in half, and hear evidence of wood knocks made by Sasquatch using large, heavy branches with which to whack repeatedly against tree trunks in "knocking" patterns as a form of communication. They also both hear and record Sasquatch vocalizations. There have been numerous examples of legitimate evidence of this kind that is professionally documented.

I was able to learn a great deal from the stories grounded in this type of evidence in a way that allowed me to piece together my own story. I was able to get a picture of Sasquatch existence in the forests. These presentations were so valuable and helpful to me. I was able to connect my Sasquatch sighting with the nightly moving shadows. —The man being on the patio and the moving shadows on the walls must be one and the same.

Also, it was at this point that I learned from the presentations to call these beings "Sasquatch People." They are a species of people who are invisible to humans unless they choose to be seen. They have been living on Earth since before our beginnings as humans. They call themselves the "Guardians of the Earth." According to other Sasquatch experiencers, the Sasquatch that have facial characteristics like humans and whose faces are covered with soft, fine hair—like the one I saw—are called the "Ancient Ones." It was an Ancient One that appeared to me at the kitchen window early that evening in March, an Ancient One.

There are different kinds of Sasquatch from different areas worldwide, and they vary in appearance. Each kind has different heights, hair color and facial features. Some Sasquatch have no facial hair, and their facial features may be more ape-like. Sasquatch can have a variety of hair colors: black, dark brown, brown, auburn and even blonde. All these different kinds fall under an overall grouping called Sasquatch.

My sighting was a stroke of good fortune, according to some of the Sasquatch research I have uncovered to date. If Sasquatch reveals himself to you, it marks the beginning of a journey of spiritual growth and development. They have chosen you for a reason. They have watched you and selected you for their teachings and healing. In March of 2018, I embarked on a grand adventure, whether I was ready or not.

Chapter Seven

Sasquatch, Are You There?

O NE DAY I NOTICED a blind, blank space the size of a half-dollar coin over the vision on my left eye. I could only see through the top part of my eye. My ophthalmologist directed me to the emergency department of the local hospital, and after an extensive check over, I was told my retina was in the process of detaching. At 10:00 AM that next morning, I was in emergency surgery, having my retina reattached. Afterward, the surgeon instructed me to keep my face pointed downward for two weeks to prevent the retina from re-detaching. I could hold my head up for only brief periods of time to eat and bathe, but all day and all night, I kept my head and face pointed down into a pillow. It was not much fun, let me tell you… Retinal issues ran in the genetics of my family. I had just joined the family club of retina problems.

I wondered if the Sasquatch People were aware of my new medical condition. It was unclear to me how much they could understand about my life. If the same question was asked of me in reverse, what I understood about the lives of the Sasquatch, my answer would be nothing. I understood nothing, even though I had read as much material as possible about them.

I followed all my doctor's orders and attended every medical follow-up appointment. After two weeks of keeping my face planted into a cube-shaped foam pillow with a big square hole in the center, I could finally hold up my head again where it belonged. Now, I could get on with my life. I was ready to move on.

After having eye to eye contact with a Sasquatch, my daily life took on a new twist. This new twist was going to take some time and fancy footwork to get used to, as I could see things were probably never going to return to normal. The shadows came to visit me regularly every night. I could see them in the room, the same as I had seen them before. They came in as moving waves of smoke speckled with round dots that could change shape like droplets of water. Odd, who would ever think Sasquatch looked quite this way.

I geared all my readings and searches on the Internet towards the positive interactions other Sasquatch experiencers and experts were having. I was grateful this kind of material was available. Their stories not only gave me hope, but they also gave me a feeling of real purpose. I made the decision to go forward with Sasquatch, although it was not clear to me just how to proceed.

At this point, I was uncomfortable talking with anyone about my experience except my husband. He realized I needed someone to talk to, so he listened carefully whenever I needed to talk about what was happening. Although he was extremely busy with the company, he remained steadfastly good to me. He understood something was going on but did not understand the nature of my new concerns. He found my stories confusing but remained patient and non-judgmental. Herein lies my soulmate, soul friend, soul husband, you name it. Jerry is remarkable to me.

It was necessary now for me to get to know Sasquatch. Basically, I had read all the information and resources available to me at hand. However, I wanted to know more; I needed to know much more. I decided to steer my search away from the conventional world in favor of the metaphysical one. The metaphysical realm, which remains largely ignored by the scientific direction our culture and society have taken, seemed like the logical step for me to take in my research. It made good sense. I had no problem going against the current scientific norms with the idea that there are just some things in our world that science cannot interpret or explain.

And that is okay. Live and let live, I say.

Besides, it was no longer working for me that Sasquatch could not exist simply because science cannot prove their existence according to the current scientific paradigm. Paradigm or not, I must now question whether our scientific methods are outdated and might benefit from a changed modality. I decided the metaphysical world would likely have an entirely different and much more useful array of information to offer.

My mind was really open now, more than it ever had been in the entirety of my life. I needed help and answers of some kind. Realizing I could not live my life secretly hiding that I had seen a different species of human existing with us in our world, I made an appointment with a professional telepathic communicator and spent a one-hour meeting asking questions.

The communicator acted as a go-between for Sasquatch and me. The session was a real eye-opener. My intuition about the shadows at night was correct—this *was* a family of Sasquatch. The Sasquatch male that appeared on the patio was a father, as well as the older, wiser elder of a group of Sasquatch that lived communally. It was this family and community that visited me at night. They had been anticipating meeting me.

Through the telepathic communicator, I carefully asked Sasquatch about the moving cloud-like shadows in the bedroom, "What are they?" Sasquatch answered, "That is us." When they were not materialized in their physical form, they took on an alternate, energetic form which was the form I saw on the walls. At night their energy looked like moving shadows or gritty smoke. They spent most of their time in this energetic form while away from home in the wilderness.

Sasquatch offered an interesting side note during the session, "We are seen by humans only if we allow it. We know when humans are around. We can live while in the wilderness, but it is getting to where we must go farther to get away from people." I learned that Sasquatch People are highly sensitive to energy, especially ours. I asked for the elder's name, but the interpreter could not pronounce it—there were too many difficult, complicated vowel sounds, although the elder Sasquatch repeated it several times when asked.

During these beginning stages of getting acquainted with Sasquatch, it was rarely apparent to me when they were present. This part was tricky and would take some work. What were the signs the Sasquatch were present anyway? They were invisible for the most part. Stumbling around in the dark about whether or not Sasquatch was present went on for a long time. After several more weeks, I began to make a little progress. I started understanding what to look for during their visits. I had no clue how to check in with them. Now, in retrospect, I realize I could have just asked them out loud to help me understand how to recognize when they were present. In my mind, however, I was talking with them without realizing it. They were listening and getting to know me.

During our getting acquainted period, I heard someone big and heavy walking up the gravel driveway several times through the open office window. Looking out of the window, I could see that no one was there, just the sound of their heavy footsteps tromping over the crushed rock surface. I assumed a Sasquatch was passing through. Maybe our driveway was part of a well-established thoroughfare used by Sasquatch People, possibly used before this area had become settled? I had no idea, but the very idea was certainly intriguing. This was a confusing time for me, but I became interested in them and wanted to be around them.

Fusty could sense them or see them—I am not sure which. Somehow, he knew when Sasquatch was nearby, as he would point his head, nose and eyes directly toward what looked like thin air to me. Sometimes, I had a strong gut feeling Sasquatch was right there with us, and Fusty was very aware of it. Whenever I found Fusty uncomfortable, I held him in my arms comfortingly. I spoke to him reassuringly, letting him know that everything was alright. I did this often, and we both slowly made our way toward a reasonable adjustment.

I WAS CHALLENGED BY my new life reality, but I accepted it and moved forward each day, step by step, as best I could. Even though I was still somewhat frightened, I put my faith in the encounters with Sasquatch and trusted what was happening around me. I strongly felt that this was important for me and my life. Something was changing for me, and I had no idea what that was. I felt a new direction was being presented, and I sensed it was good for me. I needed to trust this situation, so I did. I kept trusting this was the right thing to do.

Around that time, Jerry and I began finding the evening news too stressful, and we decided not to watch it anymore. Climate change, unprecedented unrest between the Democrats and Republicans within our government, and threats of nuclear war from dictators from various countries plagued everyday life for everyone in the world. I was hoping for help and answers from

Sasquatch. I had my fingers crossed…

I was becoming intrigued by my Sasquatch connection without a doubt, but there was a long learning curve ahead involved in trusting them rather than being fearful of them. Learning to trust Sasquatch is another matter, a new arena altogether, to put it mildly. At the same time, I was receiving guidance and healing from the Sasquatch both during dreams and telepathically. Even though I was not telepathic myself, they were able to whisper into my heart and soul what I needed to learn. I became addicted to the rich energy they fed me. I loved the growth and development taking place within me and my life. The Sasquatch were loving and benevolent beings; this gave me the courage and impetus to continue progressing forward in a relationship with them. They were both proud and pleased with the progress and changes I was making within me. It was becoming a most rewarding time.

Early one morning, while crossing the backyard to move a lawn chair, I felt someone acknowledging me proudly, the way a parent is proud of their child's accomplishments. Someone right there next to the tree where I was moving the lawn chair was feeling very proud of my progress. I did note that I was surer of myself now and more grounded as a human being. I had more confidence. I was sure it was the same elder Sasquatch man who had materialized on the patio. He was proud of my willingness for growth, development and self-awareness. I felt like I belonged. I felt like I was working with a species of humans who have answers about climate change and solutions to help humanity learn to peacefully get along together. I was creating a new life for myself, a better life with the help and support of Sasquatch. I was becoming "enlightened" by Sasquatch standards. The Sasquatch protected me, and for the first time in my life, I felt truly safe in this dark, heavy world we humans call home.

WITHIN MY NEWLY DEVELOPING relationship with Sasquatch, my education with the paranormal began at once. Several times during my learning, funny incidents came and went. I had a few humorous experiences with Sasquatch that showed they also had a sense of humor which agreed with me and brought fun and enjoyment to my life. I found myself drawn to them, hook, line, and sinker.

One late afternoon, Jerry and I sat in the living room, watching the wild birds at the feeder through the window. I had been feeling let down because the Sasquatch People seemed to have gone away. It had been a few months since they had made their presence known in our home, and I was losing hope of reconnecting with them. I could not figure out if they were around anymore and was sad and confused. I thought maybe they were gone but for how long?

I announced to Jerry that the Sasquatch and I don't hang out together anymore and that I just wish I could get to know them. I was becoming sad and missed them. I was still careful about keeping my new experiences to myself about the Sasquatch activity out of respect for Jerry's boundaries, so I was surprised when he answered, "They are around. You just can't see them." Jerry was encouraging me, and in the next moment, within close range of our hearing, a sudden and extra-loud stomach growl broadcasted loud and clear—a growl coming from a large, full-sized, hollow stomach a few feet away.

We were both startled, and we chuckled. It was timed to perfection! "See, Leanna, they ARE around!" Jerry said reassuringly. The loud stomach growl was surreal. It was uncanny a sound of that nature could pierce through the airwaves near us with no apparent visible source. I asked Jerry what that noise could be, and he answered reassuringly, "Just a sound. There are lots of sounds in life that we can't identify. That's all. It's just a sound.

Life is full of them. Don't ever let them bother you or scare you. You are perfectly safe."

This has happened several times since. Jerry was never surprised when these funny, noisy incidents occurred. He believed there were all kinds of noises out there and never gave it a second thought. He did not need an explanation for the new noises that began erupting inside the house. For Jerry, it was all just life. He tended to have such a good, sensible attitude. For me, Jerry was very comforting. He was my rock, and I was his.

Another time, we had just returned home from a trip visiting family. It was early evening when we pulled into the driveway. I was anxious to let Feller and Fusty know we were back, so I called out for them. The lions, as I liked to call them, heard me. They were approaching quickly from across the field in an exciting pattern of weaving back and forth in a switchback motion toward Jerry and me. They were fascinating to watch, and we were happy to return home and be with them again. They came into the house with us and hung out while we petted them.

Soon after, I got up and headed for the bathroom for a quick pit stop when what sounded like a colossal bee or insect buzzed loudly right past my ear. It sounded like a bumble bee ten times louder than normal and startled me good. It was unheard of that an insect that large would be inside the house, and for that matter, that any insect that large existed on the planet!

I looked around and did not find any insects. I just stood there, dumbfounded. Finally, I chuckled out loud as I realized that this was Sasquatch and their abrupt, noisy way of saying, "Hello, we're glad you are back." One thing I read about Sasquatch power is that they possess an endless array of paranormal ways of communication upon which to draw. I do not think I saw them perform one of their paranormal oddities twice. There was always something new to see and experience during their visits.

Night was a time of great activity for Sasquatch. At the Sasquatch websites I have watched, the experiencers typically approached Sasquatch during the early morning hours. That is the time when Sasquatch People are very active. There were afternoon times when they were just as busy, but Sasquatch seemed primarily nocturnal. Night after night, my bed shook as if someone had run into it. The shaking usually woke me, but it never bothered me. I never felt frightened by the jostling; I just fell back to sleep.

Sometimes, I felt someone gently touching me on my side or my shoulder. To be touched by a Sasquatch is not the same as being touched by a human. It was similar but lighter, the way the weight of a bird might feel if it were to touch your hand. The touch felt softer and more subtle. You can feel the hand or finger, but at the same time, there is no weight or density. You might receive a little picture inside your mind of the hand or finger doing the touching—they made sure you knew it was them. They meant well and were remarkably gentle.

When Sasquatch was around during daylight hours, lots of sounds went on, and I think these sounds may have been from Sasquatch children because of the playful way these antics played out. At times, when I entered the bedroom, I would hear an exact imitation of Feller making a single yowl from behind the closet door. I naturally stopped to check the closet, wondering how my cat had gotten inside. Then I would discover Feller asleep on the bed. It always made me chuckle, and I felt like the joke was on me. Feller remained fast asleep and never heard a thing. Not once did he ever respond to any Sasquatch noises. The sounds and noises may have been specifically for me. Sasquatch can do that, make sounds that only you can hear.

Another funny experience was when I heard Sasquatch imitate the sound of a haunted, squeaky door opening and closing repeatedly—the sound speeding up once they realized they had an audience. I am sure this gave them a chuckle. Jerry was with me in the kitchen eating lunch and heard it, too, but found it uninteresting and ignored it. Once again, this was simply one of life's natural sounds for Jerry. He was not startled nor impressed, but he could see I was worried. So he checked out the location of the sound for my benefit. He could see that the squeaky door had my eyes popping out of my head. He admitted that the noise sounded like a squeaky door opening and shutting, but because the sound was coming from behind the refrigerator, he dismissed it as just another sound coming from our wonderful world. Soon after, I began losing my fear and concern over loud, strange noises. It was a good lesson for me, to be sure.

Sasquatch never produced sounds that scared or upset me, though. They knew where not to go. Actually, they seemed to know me better than I did myself. They were aware that extra loud noises, for instance, really startled me. Out of consideration for how I felt, the Sasquatch were careful about the sounds they made so that they would not upset or frighten me. I have read this before about the Sasquatch in my research. They are a very advanced and intelligent race of people who can accurately read humans.

As I mentioned earlier, I heard heavy footsteps walking across the crushed rock on the driveway, and not a soul was anywhere to be seen. This happened while I was bookkeeping in the office trailer. A loud *crunch, crunch, crunch* from a set of heavy feet could be heard tromping over the gravel driveway past the office. Next, I listened to our six-foot wooden fence straining loudly under a great, invisible weight that seemed to vault up and over the top of our fence with great ease, landing loudly with two huge feet meeting the concrete patio surface on the other side, *THWACK-O*. It was amazing. That individual had cleared a six-foot fence; they must have been very athletic. I only wish I was in that great shape.

When those occurrences occurred, in my mind, I usually saw

a picture of an eight or ten-foot tall, hair-covered man hurtling over the top of our six-foot fence with great ease. It was beginning to seem reasonable that this driveway may have been a main thoroughfare of the Sasquatch and was maybe established hundreds of years ago before these five-acre plots of land were divided and sold. In fact, possibly this was a commonly used pathway by the Sasquatch before humans inhabited the northwest. I speculated away during my coffee breaks as my awe and admiration for them grew.

Another time, Fusty and I sat relaxing on the chaise lounge under a tree at the edge of the property where bushes lined the fence. We were taking a break in the cool shade and enjoying the fresh, clean-smelling air. Fusty loved having his shoulders, cheeks and chin thoroughly scratched. I stayed busy scratching while his eyes rolled up inside his head.

We were absorbed in our time together when we both heard footsteps six feet away at the edge of the bushes. Fusty quickly jumped down, predator that he was, and crouched down, waiting for the sound to occur again. He stared at the lawn where we had heard the footsteps, but nothing could be seen.

Then we heard the footsteps scuffling away and out of reach over the dry grass. Fusty crouched down again, ready to pounce. With his eyes opened wide, he pricked his ears straight up. One last time, we both heard footsteps quickly scampering away further in the distance. Fusty turned his head back and forth, trying to pinpoint the source of the scuffling feet, but the footsteps disappeared for good. I thought maybe we heard a young Sasquatch playing with Fusty. The footsteps did not sound very big, but they sounded like a human walking upright. Perhaps it was a playful child? After all, Fusty was as cute as a kitty could be. Any child would love to play with him—including a Sasquatch child. I do enjoy their sense of humor and have laughed along with them. I enjoyed it, too, that they were playful and enjoyed having fun.

Chapter Eight

Loud, Invisible Footsteps

I WAS STILL NERVOUS ABOUT venturing outdoors. I wondered why I was still scared, even though I read this was not unusual for people who have seen a Sasquatch or something extraordinary. There is a process that takes time, plenty of time. People who see things that do not exist join a club whose membership includes those who see a Sasquatch. It would take time for me to adjust to my new reality. Not only was I still undergoing mind-bending cognitive dissonance, but I also began the difficult work of reconciling what I saw, negotiating in a desperate attempt to regain equilibrium about my life. People who find themselves in this situation scramble around for a long time trying to find their footing once again. I could see Sasquatch was not going to disappear from my environment, which surprised me, so I decided it was alright—it had to be okay. There was no way back now. I simply needed time to recover from the initial shock.

I saw what I saw; there was no denying it. The adjustment

I would need to make to accommodate this change in my life was real, too real, in fact. I went through several ups and downs throughout the process of adjustment. There is a big difference between the legends and myths that Sasquatch exists versus meeting one face to face. Idea versus reality, there is a big difference here. I found out.

So, I began by picking myself up by my bootstraps each and every day and slid as gracefully as I could back into the well-worn groove of my daily routine.

One part of my daily routine was exercise, walking, to be exact. I needed to exercise but was reluctant to go outdoors now. It took a couple of weeks, but eventually, I became brave and desperate to be outdoors. So, one morning I headed out the door and up the hill for a 30-minute walk. I kept my fingers crossed that my outdoor adventure would shift me back into my comfortable and safe world with nothing out of the ordinary along the way, please! The sky was overcast and drizzly. I began the one-mile trudge uphill. Oddly, near the top was a small, isolated industrial park—a strange setting for just a few buildings. Otherwise, in this area were wetlands, chickens, donkeys and horses.

I trudged uphill and arrived near the industrial park driveway entrance, where the road curved sharply and scaled steeply up to the top of the hill. I looked forward to the breathtaking view of the Cascade Mountains to the east and the Canadian Rockies to the north, waiting for me to admire at the top. However, as soon as I rounded the curve and headed uphill, I noticed four large, excited dogs playing loudly with one another. I also noticed cars parked along the front of the buildings. It appeared that business employees brought their dogs with them and left them outside to play together to keep each other company while their owners worked.

Although I relished the idea that dogs were getting a well-deserved break and a chance at a higher quality of life, I still thought this a strange setup. I muttered to myself, "Dog leash laws were usually both respected and strictly observed, even out here in the county." I wondered how long these employees could continue turning their dogs loose at work. The dogs acted borderline out of control, and I hoped to pass by unnoticed. For the moment, they were down at the far end of the complex and did not see me pass by the entrance. The very sight of them made me wish I had just stayed home. I did not want to deal with any dogs. My nerves were hanging on by threads from my strange experiences of late. I was exhausted from the whole ordeal, and I could not imagine messing with excited dogs with my nerves jangled such as they were. It would not be good for me right now, and since dogs are sensitive creatures, they would quickly pick up on it. They may feel threatened and, in turn, threaten me. I just need the walk. I wished the dogs were not riled up; God love them.

As I was heading up the hill, the dogs spotted me. They stopped playing and began coming my way, picking up speed from the bottom end of the driveway and running roiled up in a great tangle of dogs. I could see they were not bad dogs, just overly excited dogs. The scene made me nervous, though. I felt unappreciative of their owners working away safely in a warm building; meanwhile,

I could wind up dealing with their pets to my detriment. I felt put upon. I loved dogs but did not understand them very well.

Fortunately, I had gained enough distance and was too far up the hill for the dogs. They lost interest and turned back. "Well, that was close," I told myself. A moment later, I realized that after I reached the top and admired the view of the mountains, I would need to turn around and walk back down the hill past the complex driveway on my way home.

At the top, I was distracted by the stressful situation and forgot to enjoy my reward of the view. Instead, I turned and glanced around, looking for the dogs. They were a jumble of paws, tails and yapping mouths barreling at high speed through the middle of the complex. I wished their owners would be responsible and take them inside for a while, at least until I got well beyond their reach. However, in that next instant—and in my mounting fear, I spontaneously spoke loudly inside my mind and heart, "Sasquatch People, help me with these dogs!" I was unsure whether or not a clear message was sent to the Sasquatch for help.

Afraid to start back down the hill, I waited to see if anything would happen. I hoped the Sasquatch People heard me and would help me get past these dogs. I did not know why I thought they would help me. I also wondered, "Why did I call out for them?" After all, I was still afraid to initiate contact. What made me think to ask in the first place? Desperation and fear of large, loose dogs made me call out for help…

I was careful around dogs after having been bitten at age four by Sandy, a cranky cocker spaniel in the prime of her life. In the neighborhood where I grew up, almost everyone lived in a cinder-block house. The whole town was smattered with neighborhoods consisting of cinderblock housing. Often, we were referred to as *blockheads* because of these houses.

One day in early fall, our next door neighbor was having a

party in their backyard. They were having a barbeque, and my older sister, one of her good friends from school, and I hoped we would be welcome. We entered the yard carefully. I was proud that my older sister was in kindergarten—*she had reached the big time!* Next year I, too, would be in school—*I was on top of the world.*

The neighbors warned us children about their dog, Sandy, and we were told not to *run* if she was unchained. So, we stood at the edge of their backyard and watched the people at the party. They all seemed to be having fun. After a while, my sister and her friend left, and I did not notice they had disappeared. A few minutes later, I saw Sandy's owner removing the chain from her collar. She was loose and darting around quickly.

I got scared and headed home. Although I remembered the warning, I ran out of fear of the angry, grouchy appearing dog. That was a big mistake. One moment later, Sandy ran straight for me, biting me hard and leaving a savage row of deep, painful puncture holes in the flesh of my tiny backside. A trip to the doctor for a tetanus shot immediately followed. Without a doubt, it was a day I would always remember. I have been respectful but wary of dogs since then.

I stood at the top of the hill waiting and watched as the dogs continued roughhousing along the driveway. Just as I started back down the hill, something passed over me, a gentle sensation that started at the top of my head and washed down over my shoulders. I had no idea what it was, but instantly I felt better. My confidence returned, though I wondered how that was possible, because I felt like a jangled wreck that morning. Was this the Sasquatch People? In my mind, I kept asking if it was them.

I did not understand what had happened, but my fear disappeared. I confidently headed back down the hill toward the driveway. The dogs were there, and I watched their attitude change as I got closer. They calmed down, checked me out and left. They scattered, disappearing around the corner of one of the buildings. That seemed strange, but I was relieved.

I was grateful and took a deep breath. I felt protected, as if someone or something was watching over me and keeping me safe while within reach of these dogs. What a surreal walk, and what a way to start off the day! It was puzzling. My mind was kept busy trying to understand what had just happened…?

THE NEXT DAY, I started walking back up the hill, forgetting about the dog incident only the day before. I decided it was a good day to pick up the garbage that gets tossed out of moving vehicles that drive up and down the hill. The litter lands in the ditches and on the shoulder of the road. I brought a small bag for the trash I picked up along the way. It was sad seeing it stuck in the wild rose bushes and caught up in tree branches. Once winter arrives and the trees drop their leaves, various plastic bags become air born during powerful windstorms. Some of these bags get caught amongst bare tree branches high in the air. I realized my efforts were small, but I felt I had to do something.

It was not until I reached the industrial park driveway that I remembered the dogs and stopped in my tracks. They were nowhere to be seen. I wondered if they were around. Even though yesterday had ended well, today was a new day, and facing a small pack of large, rambunctious dogs was not on my schedule, not today, not tomorrow and not any other day of the week for that matter.

Chickening out, I turned around and headed "back to the barn," as the saying goes. I began to relax and even enjoyed myself while busily picked up trash. I never did know if the dogs were there. As I headed home, I focused on all the big trees and how the sun sparkled around the leaves. They looked beautiful against the bright sunlight. I walked along, picking up garbage, engrossed in my own little world. Soon, however, I began noticing the distinct sound of large footsteps following behind me. It sounded like an extra set of feet was hitting the pavement in time with mine. I could hear gravel scatter with each step. I was startled and wondered, "Is someone following me?" I could feel my heart beating faster as my high-alert alarms began firing.

I turned and looked over my shoulder. No one was there. Concluding that the sound of the footsteps was my own, I felt slightly sheepish for being jumpy. I could not seem to block out the memory of seeing a Sasquatch that last March evening. I was still quite nervous I might see another. It was surprising how many ups and downs were part of *resolving* cognitive dissonance.

Still, my gut instinct was telling me that somewhere around nine feet behind me and on the opposite side of the road, I *was* being followed. The feet sounded big and floppy, not clumsy—just floppy.

Cognitive dissonance crept back in, squeezing my brain. I was not ready to see another species of human that could not exist. I relied on good, old-fashioned horse sense for my day-to-day functioning. Lately, however, my daily reality was fading away, clear out of sight. Seeing beings that do not exist was not part of my ordinary, predictable reality. Helplessly, I found my perceptions about the world shattering and altering once again. They were shifting like the wind-driven sands of the Sahara Desert right before my very eyes, and I feared my beliefs about life were about to turn upside-down again. I do not like topsy-turvy!

I was scared and grasped at straws about what might be happening on that lonely, isolated road. I needed courage now!

Out of self-preservation, I concluded the footsteps were my own. "I am hearing the sound of my own footsteps echoing behind me," I told myself. "I must be kicking up gravel without noticing. Echoes can turn up anywhere, especially on roads surrounded by forests."

I spoke to myself with conviction to calm my nerves and suppress my quickly mounting fright. I decided the echoes could have been created by all the moisture in the air along with the shroud of dew-laden trees. I had noticed that under certain conditions, echoes can reverberate in heavily forested areas. Sounds can bounce around, making it difficult to locate their origin. I was confident I had experienced this once or twice before, hadn't I? It was expected, quite common, in fact. There was nothing to fear.

After one deep breath of air, I started walking again, but after a short distance, I could hear the footsteps following behind me again! I also noticed the potent smell of sewer gas, an unmistakable odor. I wondered loudly in my mind if footsteps and sewer gas were following me.

Anxiously, I quickly turned to see what or who was behind me—but again, nothing was there. There was no one in sight. I wondered if a neighbor had a backed-up septic tank with the lid temporarily removed, uncovering the tank. An enormous amount of odor comes from an uncapped septic tank. The smell tends to be both penetrating and unrelenting. A couple of years ago, Jerry had our septic tank pumped. I was keenly familiar with the odor.

I combatted the fear creeping up over my entire body and forced myself to stay calm. I was scared and could feel what could be only described as my spirit trying to escape out of my body for safety. I wondered if I would pass out, but I continued walking one step at a time. After all, what could I do? I was alone on a country road in a forested area with no one around, no traffic to speak of and no houses nearby. Whatever was going to happen was going to happen. I was grateful I could pull out a teeny tiny reserve of calm from the depths of my being. After all, I had never been put through an emergency like this before.

Quickly, I headed down the hill. I guessed I had one-half mile to go before I reached home. I kept my mind off the situation and focused hard on getting out of there, but no such luck. Once again, I distinctly heard someone or something walking behind me. I was aghast when I heard these giant footsteps for the third time. I spun around with fright and irritation printed across my face. No one was there! I decided that this must be Sasquatch. I would not look over my shoulder after this and just keep walking. I wanted out of there Big-Time.

Out of nowhere, a picture of a tall, hair-covered, lanky, youthful-appearing Sasquatch powerfully shot into my brain. I was very startled and froze. I could see him in my mind. He had light, chestnut-colored hair and was somewhere well over eight feet tall. He looked young, thin and slightly shaggy. I noticed he had extra-long, bare feet. I saw him for only a couple of moments in my mind—it was confusing as he looked real, alive and within ten feet of me. At the same time, I understood that according to the world in which I was familiar, no one was actually there. No one could be there. Then I wondered if I was seeing a hologram. "Are holograms real? Am I seeing one?" I did not know. I just knew he was there, but he was not there. How could that be?

It became clear that this person-type being had been following me on the opposite side of the road and was carefully disguising his footsteps by matching them with mine. Also, it was clear that he was being careful not to scare me. The expression on his young face was of disappointment at having been caught. It appeared that he did not want me to know that he was there. I sensed he was trying to do something good, a good deed for me. He looked flustered like he had failed. I could feel great disappointment and saw his sense of self was affected by the whole incident. Somehow, I felt I let down this young person-being by not being sensitive to his goodhearted attempts to help a fellow Earth being. He was just trying to fit in. This all felt crazy and confusing, but I could sense this being was trying to do something good.

After that, I was embarrassed for being so cowardly. This was such an unusually emotional and confusing circumstance I found myself in. I stopped feeling frightened and began feeling compassion for this tall, shaggy youth. Even though he was covered with hair, I could see he was some kind of human. I lost my fear of him. I could see he was very harmless. He was certainly large and somewhat scary looking, but he came off as very gentle and harmless. It would have been appropriate for me to console him...—After all, he appeared young and vulnerable.

After I saw the picture of the tall, young Sasquatch inside my mind, the footsteps stopped altogether. They quit following me. Although, the permeating odor of gas followed me all the way up to the front door. This walk up the hill qualified as a day of high strangeness, to say the very least.

I SPOKE WITH JERRY about my walks up the hill and asked if he had smelled the sewer gas. He said he had not but listened to my story with his usual patience and support. I appreciated him and his unwavering kindness to me. I was having extraordinary experiences—at least I had my husband with whom to discuss what was going on in my life. This gave me solace. I felt closer to him now more than ever.

A few months later, I decided to talk with the telepathic communicator again. This time I had questions about the incident involving the large dogs. I wanted to clarify what had taken place. The telepathic communicator welcomed my appointment. I felt grateful that I had found someone I could count on if I had questions or wanted to learn more. When the Sasquatch People were asked about the incident at the top of the hill, their answer surprised me. They had heard me call for them, and they came quickly to help me. They further explained that they would help me whenever I needed them. That was interesting, to put it mildly. "Help me whenever I need them? What kind of beings are these?"

My next question was about the sensation on the top of my head, and what made the dogs calm down? The elder Sasquatch who I saw on the patio explained that they had changed my energy into Sasquatch energy. "What is Sasquatch energy?" I asked him. "One-with-nature energy," he answered. He further explained that I would be safe around dogs now. The whole community of Sasquatch all chuckled, and the elder Sasquatch let me know that now deer and coyotes would love me!

My mind began ticking with more questions than I could keep track of. I asked them about wild animals in wilderness areas. I wondered about wolves and bears—did the Sasquatch People have conflict or problems with them? This elder Sasquatch answered that they are not afraid of wolves or bears, and by the same token, wolves and bears are not fearful of them—another interesting answer for sure. Sometimes they see bears and wolves in the forests, but they live in harmony with these two powerful predators. The Sasquatch do not bother the bears and wolves, and the bears and wolves do not bother them. But yes, they occupy some of the same wilderness areas.

I asked them about our local pack of coyotes that run around howling during the night. Were my two cats safe? I had often worried about Feller and Fusty—I didn't want them to have a run-in with coyotes. The telepathic communicator asked, "They want to know if you want them to protect your cats from the coyotes?" Quickly, I answered, "Really? Yes, I do!" At that point, I felt someone was in my court looking out for my cats and me. Could life get any better?

AFTER THIS QUESTION-AND-ANSWER SESSION with Sasquatch, I noticed dogs acted differently around me; for the most part, they avoided me. One day, Jerry and I took our Ford F-150 in for servicing, and I had an unusual encounter with two dogs at the auto repair shop. The owner had a sweet Rottweiler and a somewhat aggressive Jack Russell Terrier mix. The Rottweiler was sweet and friendly towards me, and the terrier mix was even more social. He jumped on my lap as I sat on the couch in the customer waiting room. He started playing and cuddling with me. The owner watched for a few minutes with some concern and warned me that this terrier had bitten a few customers in the past. He impressed upon me that this dog should not be trusted. I worried after the owner left, as I had no idea how to deal with the terrier on my lap. I suppose I could have stood up, and the dog would have had to jump down. I must confess here and now: I am a cat mom. I understand cat protocol as well as I know anything. Dogs, they are another matter. I love them dearly, though. I just do not understand them.

Next, I noticed the big Rottweiler was shaken and left, sliding away into an adjoining room. That seemed odd to me...

Honestly, I was unsure how to get the terrier off my lap. I did not grow up with dogs, but I kept playing with him, hoping for the best. He seemed perfectly happy and excited with me. The owner checked up on us a few times to make sure the small dog was still behaving.

When our truck was ready, the shop owner returned to write a repair invoice and check on the dogs. He was surprised to find that the Rottweiler was hiding away from me, visibly anxious. He was let outdoors and disappeared behind the house on the property. "Well, what do you know about that?" said the owner, scratching his head. "He isn't usually afraid of people. He's usually overly friendly and playful."

He glanced over at the terrier in my lap and commented, "I don't know about that either. I was worried he would bite you. He has done that in the past." This terrier seemed to just love me. I did not feel threatened by him any more than I did by the sweet Rottweiler.

After a few months went by, I decided it was time to contact the telepathic communicator and get set up to ask for more information from Sasquatch. I still had questions about dogs, so during the session, I specifically requested additional clarification about my interactions with them. I noticed that more aggressive or alpha dogs either liked or tolerated me. Friendly, submissive dogs avoided me. When I asked if this was a result of the one-with-nature energy I now possessed, the elder Sasquatch answered, "Yes. It is the one-with-nature energy dogs are sensing." When asked why that was, he explained, "Dogs are raised by humans to relate to humans. They are trained to tune into their owner's energy. My one-with-nature energy feels unfamiliar to them, and they cannot tune into it. It makes them uncomfortable." I have noticed over the years that dogs will avoid situations that make them uncomfortable. They do not stick around.

After that session, I felt perfectly safe around dogs. I was able to keep a respectful distance from them. Now, when I pass dogs on park trails during walks, I go unnoticed. I respect their space by keeping my eyes to myself. I think it is an issue of space with dogs, so I stay away from theirs. I feel quite safe in their presence, a great feeling indeed.

I have yet to test whether or not coyotes love me. Jerry and I hear the coyotes at night but rarely see them. The deer no longer seem afraid of me. They behave as though I am not a threat whatsoever. I must remind them every now and again to stay out of our backyard and gardens.

My policy has always been to keep a healthy distance from wild animals. I have never thought it a wise idea to live very near them. They have their place, and we have ours. I have read articles about diseases jumping from animals to humans and vice versa. It has never seemed right to me that we live closely together.

I saw my life improving. I realized now that I had a species of very tall people with extraordinary powers there for me if I needed them. This was the beginning of the Sasquatch People becoming my people and me theirs, the beginning of a tight bond of love, loyalty, friendship and family. At this time, I began to feel like the luckiest human in the whole wide world.

Chapter Nine

More Sasquatch!

T IME MARCHES ON AND waits for no man, as they say. Jerry and I plugged along with the company. We started and finished job after job, paid our employees, suppliers and vendors, and we always paid the Feds. Our life was like clockwork. We were working our way through another summer, the time of year we were the busiest. I planted my garden and enjoyed watching the seeds sprout and develop into lovely plants.

Each year I learned more about feeding the garden soil to encourage a whole range of nutrients from microbes all the way up to centipedes and pill bugs throughout the garden beds. I watched for different types of insects to regularly visit and enjoy the variety of flower pollens and nectars from the flowering plants. Numerous kinds of wasps, flies and bees visited the garden daily. This was an essential part of gardening, and I looked forward to the insect life every year.

The weather this summer was promising. In the garden area

surrounding the upper patio, I filled the beds with tall, colorful sunflowers with broad, flowering heads to create cool shade below. Below the flowers was our outdoor table and chairs. Each morning I came out as early as 4 AM to drink my tea and watch the sunrise. During the heat of the day, it was a cool and peaceful place to sit and contemplate life. It was here that I made most of my important decisions.

As I began to feel more comfortable with the new "strangeness" in my life, I decided it was time to contact Sasquatch on my own terms. I made another appointment to meet with the telepathic communicator to talk with the elder Sasquatch, the leader of the community with whom I had a connection. It bothered me that I had no name or title to use while talking with him. Using his name was an important gesture of respect, as I wanted him to know how good I felt about our growing friendship.

That whole week I had been searching for a name he might accept for me to use while addressing him personally. The telepathic reader and I could never make heads or tails out of the combination of vowel sounds that made up his given name. I came up with the name Mannie. I liked the name and felt it would be an appropriate, friendly name for him. So, during that session with the Sasquatch, I asked the elder Sasquatch man if I could call him Mannie since I could not pronounce his real name. The interpreter told me, "Yes, he likes that name." My heart surged with unconditional love from Mannie, and my face beamed with a smile that reached from ear to ear. I felt a powerful connection with Mannie.

LATER THAT WEEK, I ran across an interesting blog about a Sasquatch experiencer who was having positive interactions with a local community of Sasquatch. The blog described a technique they used to connect with Sasquatch to actually see them. The method was outlined in a few simple steps.

One night I performed the technique presented in the blog. I decided I wanted to see Sasquatch for myself. There were a few simple steps involved, which I followed and was apparently successful. I was not expecting to see anything at all and was surprised when later that evening, I saw a face appear on the bedroom wall in the dark. I could see a simple outline of hair, eyes, eyebrows, nose and mouth. The outline was like a crude, primitive sketch, and the medium used for the portrait was a yellowish, dull light. The face was forming right on the wall. The nose and mouth were not as clear but were placed correctly on the face. Also, the face was energized with tiny, bright flecks of white light that were winking out at me.

I was startled. Momentarily, another face appeared identical to the first. The two faces were side by side on the wall, just above the bed, where I could see them plainly. Then another and another, until four faces peered at me from the wall—four, two-dimensional, pale-mustard-colored face outlines were grouped together on the wall. Although strangely, they were on the wall, yet they were not on the wall—they were floating within millimeters of the surface of the wall. That would be much more accurate.

It was surreal and frightened me—as if a science-fiction movie overlapped my daily life. I shut my eyes and could not reopen them. Cognitive dissonance, my old friend, once again made my brain ache with shock and confusion. I blamed myself and felt I had exposed myself to a world I could not understand and probably never would, for that matter. It seemed I had overreached and was too far outside my comfort zone. I had made a mistake. I applied the technique to attempt contact with Sasquatch, and it worked. I could see them, and they could see me. Oh, my lord…

now what do I do? I did not know who or what kind of beings these people were, nor what had I gotten myself into. Once again, I assumed this was Sasquatch...

Seeing tends to be believing. Now, I was back to coping with the complications of deep cultural shock—the shock that there might be another species of people living on our planet. I had seen them. This was a hard one for me, the idea that another human species could live here on Earth. I assumed that these were Sasquatch, but I could not be entirely sure. This was as close to the truth as I felt I could get. My zeal for life sunk back into the familiar hopeless abyss I dwelled in after seeing the hair-covered man on the patio. Each time I took a step forward, it seemed as though I slid back two more in shock and dismay. I needed to hide from life and felt desperate once again. My mind ached as it was thrust back into conflict. I had seen the Sasquatch, but it was almost more terrifying than what I had seen on the patio. I remained in this conflicted state for weeks, as my head was swimming in complete and thorough disbelief.

EVENTUALLY, I CONFIDED TO Jerry what was going on. It must have been rough for him, hearing me discuss something both controversial and fantastical in such a desperate way. Kindly he reminded me that I can see more than most people, and that is okay. He exclaimed how lucky I was and that most other people were not seeing as much as they should. He turned it around to make me feel better. He was so good to me. I was grateful to him even more than ever...

While reflecting on my new experience, I realized no one wanted to hear or talk about Sasquatch. No one that I knew, anyway. Denial was my safety valve, so I refused to believe I had seen anything. Just a blob of mustard or chunk of ham, something that upsets the stomach and plays tricks on the eyes, as the character

Ebenezer Scrooge rationalized after having seen the spirit of Jacob Marley in Charles Dickens's famous novel, *A Christmas Carol*. I was simply having gastronomic symptoms which affect the "senses" after eating certain foods. Downplaying my experiences was the only relief I could find at that time.

Over the next few weeks, I caught glimpses of the faces on the same wall again. Fearfully, I shut my eyes and could not open them. One night while tentatively glancing around the room, I saw two full-body outlines with faces across the room on the closet doors. The figures were approximately six feet tall.

Shocked and dismayed, I sealed my eyes shut again. Then a tapping sound started up from that general area—an insistent but gentle tapping, like someone using a pen tip trying to get my attention. The tapping spread from the closet doors and over onto the wall, where I had seen the four faces earlier. Part of me wanted to laugh because a tapping was coming from my right side on the wall and from the closet beyond my feet. It was so far removed from reality for a sound to come from a wall or a door. Insistently, someone was trying to get me to look at them. Someone persistently wanted my attention.

I did not look. I was too afraid, but I did chuckle at the absurdity of it all. Then, I started to feel very bad that I was letting someone down by not looking. It felt like an adolescent was trying to get my attention, but I would not give it to them. It was just too strange. My heart sank into that sad place you find yourself when you let down someone you genuinely care for. I wanted to cry but could not open my eyes—a very sad end to that day.

Jerry never heard any of the tapping sounds. He could not see any of the outlines I described to him. It was rough, but I had to just keep going. There seemed to be no other choice. Somehow, I was confident that everything would make sense to me. I just stayed in the moment, day by day.

As time wore on and the faces continued to appear, I surprised myself by becoming comfortable with them. I enjoyed them visiting me from the wall. The primitive artwork was always the same. The portraits looked like crude sketches with facial features in their proper and respective places on the faces. In a few months, I became overjoyed to see them and got acquainted with what appeared to be the Sasquatch family I had been in contact with for a while now. There was a mother, father, children and other adults. I do not know precisely how many, but I would estimate around 30 people in this community. I looked forward to seeing them and missed them if they did not appear. I noticed they came in March and stayed through the end of November. They were gone over the winter until spring. I came to miss them very much when they were gone.

I learned to feel Sasquatch energy. It was very gentle while they were in spirit form. There was a lovely, calm gentleness and a complete naturalness to them when they were present. After each visit, I felt secure and included in their community. My mind was really open to the experience of them. They were very good people, and I wanted to be with them more.

However, sometimes during their visits with me on the wall at night, their energy was an altogether new situation that needed resolving. At certain times the energy emitting from the mustard light portraits was powerful, so powerful that I could visit for only short spurts of time. I could look at the faces, but my eyes would not focus very well and would tire quickly. My body could barely take the energy, and I would fall asleep. I did not want to miss out on anything. The energy was almost as strong as the energy Mannie, the hair-covered man was emitting that night on the patio. A strong urge to sleep usually overcame me.

Sasquatch energy is not like ours. I learned from my research that they vibrate at a much higher and faster rate. This made it difficult for me to be with them for very long periods of time. They knew this, too. Somehow, I knew they could see the effect their presence was having on me physically. However, in my mind, we were hitting it off and enjoying the company of one another, an unexpected outcome for sure.

I have since learned that our energy vibrates at a much lower, slower and denser rate. Our energy feels very heavy to the Sasquatch. Sometimes, they cannot take our energy either, especially if we are particularly loaded with problems—heavy baggage, as we call it. We do not necessarily feel good to Sasquatch.

Early during their nightly visits, some Sasquatch family members showed me different and interesting things. They held a presentation for me on the wall one evening that I really enjoyed. The presentation was illustrated in light; however, the light was not yellow. The light was white.

Utilizing their paranormal powers, what I believe was an adolescent Sasquatch began a projection on the wall, approximately 13" square or so. At first, I could see blacker-than-black shadows building up within the 13" space, and then an image began to form in the white light. Having never seen this kind of light before, I named it "spirit light."

I strained my eyes to watch while the intense high energy from Sasquatch presence pressured my body to fall asleep—I fought it off for as long as I could, as I did not want to miss out. Meanwhile, a succession of different animal profiles, one after another, projected like a slide show onto the wall. The projection of each animal was just the head, and each animal's head was visible for about 40 seconds. Then the next animal portrait began forming and took its place. All the animals appeared to be predatory, like bears and wolves; however, they did not look like bears or wolves. They were different. One of the animals looked like a cross between a wolf and a bear, I guess you could say, and some had a cougar-like appearance. I viewed several different wild animals and could not determine what part of the animal kingdom any of them belonged to. None of them were familiar, but they looked real—like authentic, legitimate wild animals, except they were all foreign to me.

It was fascinating. I was seeing something I believed no one had ever seen before. The sense of Sasquatch sharing their world with me pervaded and filled the room. The young Sasquatch wanted to share with me. They were proud of their wild animals, and I was proud to be their audience. These engaging youths and their world left a lasting impression on me. The show ended, and I fell right to sleep, awestruck.

During this time, Sasquatch showed a great deal of interest in me. Several young Sasquatch visited me and showed me different things I understood were vital to them. I saw in these youths the same emotional stages my own children underwent during their teenage years. I saw the sharing as an essential part of them becoming adults, Sasquatch adults. It is usual for adolescents to be interested in new things, as they need experiences. I believed they were looking forward to and preparing for their future lives as adults, just as high school seniors do in our school systems. I was very moved that they were sharing their hopes and dreams with me. These adolescents were innocent and appeared to be trying new things. They were precious and vulnerable like all children everywhere.

I figured the adolescents were interested in me because they most likely had never connected with a human before. I must have been an anomaly. I was so aware of them, and more than seeing the facial sketch on the wall, I could feel their hearts and souls yearning to grow and develop, yearning to understand their world and how to fit in. This is not unlike our own children as they grow into adults. These adolescents knew I could see them.

I suspected this was a new and rare experience for the Sasquatch living in my area.

I did not know how to interact with them, so I watched them quietly, politely and lovingly. As a dedicated mother with two grown children of my own, I had always felt that the youth of the world were our future. All youth need to be nurtured through their maturity process. They need support to become the capable and happy contributing citizens they were meant to be within their respective communities. I will say it again, *ALL* of our youth are our future, no matter who they are or where and how they live.

I embraced the Sasquatch youths wholeheartedly as if they were my own children. By this time, they were present with me often. I was not afraid of the images on the wall and was interested in what was going on in their lives. It mattered. These were young people with a future. I felt some degree of responsibility for them, but I had no clue what that responsibility could be, which was gut-wrenching. I cared about them very much.

The energy surrounding my interactions with the adolescents continued to grow. The sketches became more elaborate, and I could see them moving and changing. There were a lot of self-portraits marked out on the wall for me to see. The picture would last only a few moments and begin fading. Next, the wall would get very black, and a new image began to form, an image of whatever seemed important to that youth. Sometimes, there were symbols and pictures I did not always understand—these may have been some of the things they saw during their daily lives. All our youth, Sasquatch youth included, are looking for the same emotional aspirations for their future. These youngsters presented themselves like typical young people—full of optimism and with their whole life ahead of them.

A few nights later, a fascinating dark shadow began to form on the wall. It was details of an individual's face. Surprisingly, the face pushed forward through the wall. I could see a young male Sasquatch in the flesh, looking straight at me—just his face.

He was looking at me, showing himself to me from somewhere. Not from inside the wall, but from where? He was coming from somewhere because I could see the background. I could see the natural surroundings behind him. Astonishment would only graze the surface of how shocking this was. He was there for a few moments and then was gone. Speechless, I was left speechless…

I noted that his face was not covered with hair. The young Sasquatch had an expressive face, and I could easily see that he was pretty sensitive. I saw he was capable of the entire range of feelings expressed by human teenagers: a little rebelliousness, deep passion and great curiosity about the world, for starters. His facial features looked almost 100% human, only slightly longer. He had a slightly longer nose, face, and head.

He did not look like an ape the way the Internet depicts Sasquatch. He was human—that I did not expect. He did not look fierce or scary. He was there for only a few moments, a fine-looking young Sasquatch male. To me, he looked about 14 years old. I was surprised by his trust in me and was completely honored to meet him face-to-face. I did not take this honor and trust lightly.

SOMETIMES THE SASQUATCH YOUTH played practical jokes during the presentations. While their faces were outlined on the wall, they would comically switch up the facial features by rearranging them on their faces. They must have found this particularly funny because they did it often. Their mouth would intentionally be placed above the eyes, or their mouth and nose would trade places. Many times, they turned their mouths wrong-side-up and even sideways—this was one of their favorite jokes. A line of faces with features placed in different positions was a common joke. I could feel them expecting me to be shocked by their special effects, but I would gently chuckle, enjoying Sasquatch humor. These were indeed teenagers!

A short while later, one young teenager took things a step further. I could see him in the mustard light against the door with the word "Hi" spelled out in white light inside a box of light. He held the box up between his two hands for me to see. It was like he was holding up a flash card made of pale light—like a greeting card, so to speak. "How ingenious," I thought.

A few moments later, he spelled out a name—Steffins—in light within the box. He held this up for me to see. This teenager's name was Steffins. What a wonderful and youthful name, indeed! At that moment, I connected the young teenage boy who pushed his face forward through the wall to this Sasquatch youth, spelling his name for me. He was introducing himself. This was an introduction to Steffins!

Even though I was stunned, I was filled with unexpected emotion and respect for this young Sasquatch male. I realized all at once that this race of beings could spell—and if they could spell, they could communicate. *We* could communicate. Then the irresistible urge to fall asleep became a battle, and I lost. I considered this an obstacle in our getting acquainted because the power emitting from the youth was more than I could take. I believe they understood this but never held it against me. Sadly, I was not able to respond. However, the fact that I did not respond did not deter any efforts to connect with me on their part.

After I received the message from Steffins, I took it upon myself to draw a picture on a sheet of paper for all the Sasquatch People to see. I drew simple stick figures of Jerry, me, Feller and Fusty. I made the stick figures wave their hands and wrote, "Hi." I sketched hearts connecting the four of us together. I wrote "Family." Then I wrote our names beneath each figure. I taped the picture face-out on the inside of the kitchen window where I had seen Sasquatch for the first time and displayed it there for all to see when they arrived in the evening to visit.

Afterward, the bedroom wall at night remained a real happening place. It was wonderful, and I came to look forward to nighttime and visiting with the Sasquatch. It was the high point of each and every day, and then one night, it ended. A week went by, and I saw no sign of Sasquatch. I felt heartsick, soul sick. I wondered if maybe the Sasquatch had moved on. I missed them so badly that my heart ached. Nobody came to visit me anymore. I became sad and eventually, my heart started to break.

One day, while I was sad and bewildered, I wondered loudly inside my mind what had happened to the Sasquatch People? Where did they go? Why were they gone? Overwhelmed with grief, I dropped my face into my hands and wept. It surprised me just how heartbroken I was. I thought they were gone and I would never see them again. I would miss them grievously. They did not owe me anything, but I had grown attached to them.

The next day, a Sasquatch youth appeared on the closet door outlined in the usual yellowish light. With great surprise, I perked up and was glad to see a Sasquatch. This individual began sending me light in the shape of hearts. He held the hearts up between his two hands, and they flowed straight out towards me like overlapping coiled wire. I watched in utter amazement. I felt unconditional love emanating from the Sasquatch youth reassuringly. The adolescent seemed stressed out that I had reached the wrong conclusion. Once again, I was stunned but pleased.

Evidently, I had the wrong impression, and this youth was here to set me straight about our relationship. I was terribly moved and realized there was much more to learn about these people. They are people with deep feelings, more profound and more pure than ours. Now, they really felt like family to me. By this time, I wanted to be considered a member of their community. I believed they accepted me as family. This was becoming the experience of a lifetime.

It was hitting home for me that the Sasquatch People are genuinely here for us human beings. I had read often in my research about Sasquatch and their unconditional love. I was beginning to see the truth in what I had read because I was having personal experiences with it now myself. It was changing my life and giving me so much confidence, more confidence than I had ever experienced before. I wanted to learn to be that same way toward others. Lord knows we need to treat each other better. We deserve so much better from each other. I wanted to be a more loving person, just like Sasquatch. I wanted to start making a difference in the world.

I always enjoyed it when the young Sasquatch came to visit because there were new and exciting things to experience. I did not always understand their pictures. One day I was shown two cat faces that morphed and turned into empty skulls—the eyes were black holes, and the mouths were black slits. Startled and frightened, I shut my eyes. I could not face what they were showing me.

The next night, I was shown the same two skulls. I became instantly aware that they were trying to tell me my cats would pass away. I wondered if they were an advanced species of people who could see into the future. It was more than I was willing to face or process. I did not allow myself to acknowledge the skulls. I ignored them by turning away for the night and falling asleep.

Meanwhile, spring was turning into summer. The garden was coming along nicely. Work flowed smoothly for Jerry each day. We got paid, the crew got paid, and we never looked back with a single regret. We paid good attention to the cats, and together Jerry and I shared our stories into the evening.

Our company was a lot of responsibility for just two people.

We were constantly busy and could not take time off to travel except for short jaunts to see family. But even though we could not take vacations, there was still so much to look forward to in the summer months. It was a great time of year.

Chapter Ten

Footsteps in the Dark

O NE OF MY MOST memorable encounters was when I heard Sasquatch walk right up to me. One very dark evening in late fall, I stepped out onto the porch to gaze up at the stars. As I watched the sky, I heard a couple of loud, brittle branches snapping underfoot about 100 yards off in the dark woods beyond the fence.

I suspected that this was Sasquatch and not a random sound. "Uh-oh," I trembled. "If this is Sasquatch, I will be afraid out here alone in the dark." I steeled myself to maintain composure and stood out on the porch facing the direction of the occasional snapping branch. I listened intently. I could hear footsteps slowly coming my way. It sounded like it could be a Sasquatch, but a small one—maybe a child based on the faint-sounding footfalls I was hearing. The movements were tentative, as if stepping slowly, carefully choosing a trail.

As the footsteps got closer, I noted that there was no sound from the tree branches that were low, hanging, and blocking the way into my yard. They remained silent as if undisturbed. The branches were not moving nor making any sound, no swooshing or swishing noise anywhere, even though they were blocking the path. But the footsteps were coming closer, coming directly towards me through the wall of brush and tree branches. I wondered, "How was this possible that only the sound of the footsteps could be heard? Why was the sound of tree branches and brush sounds not present?" Tree branches and bushes make a distinct noise when they are pushed aside.

It was too much and too strange. I became overwhelmed. It was becoming clear that Sasquatch could walk right through trees and brush silently. I found this unnerving. The ordeal was getting into the paranormal, the area where I had little experience and no confidence.

Standing on the dark porch, I tried ever so hard not to be afraid. By now, I knew it was a Sasquatch and that I was safe, but at this point, I had never had anyone, let alone a Sasquatch walk toward me outdoors at night. I was wary of the dark and the footsteps that were approaching.

I was not sure what I would do next, but then I heard footsteps effortlessly closing in through the wall of tangled blackberry vines, easily, silently. I felt the hair along my scalp prickle as I listened, debating when to run back into the house through the front door. Would I be able to open the door? Would my hands still work? I hoped my brain would stay engaged, so I could open the door and get inside the house.

After the thorny wall of blackberries was passed through, the bushy Camellia tree, which was lodged tightly against the split rail fencing, was all that was left between the approaching Sasquatch and me. Blackberry brambles were mashing the Camellia against the fence like a tin of sardines. They were the last obstacle between me on the dark porch and the approaching Sasquatch. The blackberry had dozens of thorny vines which stretched upward, out, and over the top of the Camellia tree and hung suspended in mid-air, forever reaching and threatening to invade our yard in their never-ending quest to take over our world. I held my breath as I waited and watched on high alert.

The Sasquatch passed through the Camellia without a sound. I heard footsteps stop in the grass right in front of me on the porch. The Sasquatch, after having walked silently through the brush, blackberries and tree without making a sound, was standing in front of me in the wet grass. I was too stunned. That was too much paranormal activity for me.

A chilling fear began at the top of my head and crept down over my face, neck and chest. This was becoming more than I could take. I was about to fail this test of courage I believed was being presented to me by the Sasquatch People. Deep inside, I had a great desire to let go of fear and live life confidently. As a highly sensitive species of beings, the Sasquatch were aware of my aspirations and were attempting to help me overcome my fears with an outdoor opportunity for the experience. Even though they were gentle and careful throughout the experiment, it was too much for me. I was going to fail the test.

The young Sasquatch was standing about twelve feet away. I could not see him but could hear that he had pressed forward beyond the woods and was standing in the wet grass facing me. I tried in vain to make out any details of a Sasquatch individual, but there was no moonlight, and there was nothing to be seen. There was just the darkness of the night.

Even though I knew an individual Sasquatch was standing right there in front of me and that I was not in any danger, I was ready to bolt. I was terrified, as if all my nightmares were coming true, ghosts were real, and there really were extraterrestrial beings living among us. I was quickly coming to the realization that there was more to our universe than I could ever wrap my brain around.

Not wanting to play a part in a science-fiction story about aliens and UFOs, nor a scene from *The Invisible Man,* I dashed across the porch and threw open the door. Instantly, I felt okay. I was home safe. For some reason, I felt safe inside the house, even though I knew the walls meant nothing to Sasquatch. They could see through walls and walk right through them.

In the end, this was a missed opportunity for me to connect with Sasquatch on a physical level. I was disappointed and hoped I would feel safer next time and could learn to be outdoors with them. Many other Sasquatch experiencers spend time outdoors, where more physical interactions can occur.

AT THAT POINT, I pieced together the impossibility of wild animals overcoming their fear of humans. I could see how hopeless it was for them. Ingrained fear can be so rock-hard. I figured that fear is just part of the brain's hard wiring for all creatures that exist on Earth and is natural. The Sasquatch People had given me an opportunity—I hoped I had not let them down.

Sasquatch realizes humans have fears and they are trying to understand us better. They do not live in fear, so it is curious to them that we do. Part of our healing process as humans is getting past fear—an excellent goal. If we can overcome fearfulness, imagine what would take its place—confidence and freedom to live!

My paranormal interactions with Sasquatch remain ongoing. At the very least, these interactions are the most exciting part of my life. I am becoming slightly more tuned in to the complexity of their quantum-level powers now. There is always something new to experience with them.

Chapter Eleven

Unexplainable Wildlife Camera Photos

F OR CHRISTMAS IN 2018, Jerry and I decided to buy a wildlife trail camera as a gift for ourselves. We were interested in mounting one on a tree that faced beyond our fence over the vast hayfields where the cats roamed and hunted. We were curious about the passing nighttime wildlife. This was when the fun began.

For the next year and a half, Jerry and I spent a little time together each morning in our robes with our big mugs of tea on the couch, watching videos taken during the night. We discovered actual wildlife crossing through the pathway of the camera lens, including the cats! We found that our cats were filmed numerous times. This was nothing out of the ordinary in the general sense, but as proud cat stage parents, we were delighted and found it extraordinary! We could see what our cats were up to during the night. It was a different world altogether.

We never grew tired of seeing Feller and Fusty hunting and returning home through the holes cut in the wire fence. One video filmed Fusty carrying a dead mouse into the backyard. The film showed him stopping to shake the water from wet grass off his paws. He was fussy and did not enjoy getting his feet wet; he was a fastidious soul, through and through.

Feller was a natural, 'wildish' cat that accepted nature and all its weather conditions. We often caught him on film dashing through the long, rain-soaked hay and past the camera lens darting for cover. His instincts kept him from exposing himself out in the open for any length of time. He was aware of the coyote pack and naturally knew when they were around. I hoped he taught Fusty all there was to know about coyotes, and I hoped the Sasquatch People were protecting the cats too.

Jerry had made three strategic cuts in the wire fence, just large enough for a cat to slip through if a fast escape was necessary. Often, when I heard coyotes out in the back fields, I called the cats inside and kept them in the house for the night. When they were young kittens, I tried to make them indoor cats, but it was not their destiny to live indoors. Lord knows I tried. I was worried about the coyotes that I heard in the middle of the night, which created my concern for their well-being. Alas, they were outdoor cats, and there was nothing I could do to change that.

This camera introduced us to a number of our wildlife neighbors. There was a herd of deer, a small pack of coyotes, a raccoon, different owls, bats, insects and more. We were hoping maybe to see a newborn fawn in the spring. Also, the video camera picked up all the nighttime sounds. Frequently, we heard trains passing by on the railroad tracks a few hundred yards off. Airplanes were also captured on video silently landing at the airport nearby. It was all so exciting and fun.

IT WAS TIME FOR Jerry and me to stop working. We were getting tired and were past retirement age. Jerry was trying to sell our company and was looking to find someone local to take over and continue doing commercial remodels in the area. Fortunately, that next February 2019, Jerry was able to find a buyer for our construction company. At the point of sale, I retired immediately, and the new bookkeeper took over that day. Jerry needed to continue working through September and finish the tenant improvements in a downtown apartment complex. Relief was on the way for us, as we were burned out. Jerry was 70 years old, and I was just a few years behind. We were relieved our work life would soon be ending. We were ready for a less stressful life.

We continued enjoying our morning ritual of tea, bathrobes and the trail camera videos. Early on in my research, I had read about Sasquatch and cameras—that Sasquatch did not want any pictures taken of them. A few different websites went on to explain that they were aware of cameras and avoided them.

I tried to make my intentions clear to the Sasquatch, talking to them inside my mind, letting them know where our camera was mounted. I wanted to make it clear to Sasquatch that the camera was meant for wildlife, and they would get their picture taken if they got in front of it. So, whenever I removed and reinstalled the photo memory card, I worked at imprinting in my mind this message to Sasquatch.

I was working hard, learning to talk to them inside my mind as if we were conversing. I used my intentions to make it clear to them what the camera was all about—although, at that time, I had no idea if they were getting the messages like I had hoped. I really did not know. My whole feeling had been to respect their wishes and, at the same time, protect their privacy. My goal was to develop a trusting relationship with Sasquatch. It mattered a great deal to me.

OVER THE COURSE OF that year, we captured pictures of deer, coyotes and the cats. The videos enabled us to watch all their nightly movements. One freezing cold morning, we captured a video of what looked like bubbles drifting up through the tree branches and alongside the legs and feet of grazing deer. The deer did not appear to see them, so we thought the bubbles were camera artifacts, something occurring internally inside the camera and caused by the cold temperatures or moisture.

The video camera was picking up baseball-sized bubbles—and when a wind came up, the bubbles drifted in the direction of the breeze. Sometimes the bubbles drifted right smack into the camera, growing larger as they got closer. We shifted our attention from the cats and deer to these peculiar, drifting bubbles. They were intriguing.

During some of my reading about Sasquatch, I learned that orbs are a phenomenon related to Sasquatch presence. Our bubbles did not quite look like the orbs pictured in the photos. Ours were transparent or opaque and moved the way bubbles would be expected to move—floating and drifting. The orbs I found in pictures during my research did not appear clear but seemed more complicated, with intricate details within each sphere. I did not know how these orbs moved because they were still pictures.

However, our video camera picked up the bubbles on film each morning. I drew the conclusion they were not visible to the naked eye. The orb-like bubbles showed up during the early hours of each morning video.

We grew fascinated and hoped each morning we would find more to observe. The number of bubbles increased as our interest increased. Soon, there were hundreds and hundreds pouring out from the branches of the trees in the background. Huge wafts of bubbles poured out of the trees every night. We did not understand the nature of these bubbles, but we could see them clearly on video.

Then one night, when no wind was present, we noticed the bubbles drifted upward into the trees; others drifted along the tops of the tall grass. Some looked like they were weaving between the legs of the standing deer, and as I mentioned earlier, the deer were never aware of them. Jerry thought it curious these bubbles could travel upward from the ground. They did not always travel downward. At times, it appeared they had a mind of their own and controlled which way they traveled. I drew the conclusion that what we were seeing were orbs, orbs related to Sasquatch presence and not bubbles or camera artifacts.

Spring arrived, and so did a fawn! The camera picked up a tiny, spotted fawn leaping up and over the tall hay alongside its mother. It was beautiful. We loved all the videos of the fawn and watched it grow and become steadier over time.

Focusing on the deer, we lost interest in the orbs. Some of our footage of the doe and fawn was spectacular. In one video, the grazing doe triggered the camera, and the video started rolling. Suddenly, out from the side of the video frame, the fawn shot past its mother at top speed, disappearing out of sight beyond the camera lens. The fawn was so fast; its passing happened in just seconds. We guessed the fawn was practicing the life skills it would need to outrun predators and survive in the world.

WORK AT THE APARTMENTS continued for Jerry through summer, and finally, September arrived. At long last, he reached his final day, the last morning he would need to get up early and go to work. Owning and operating a commercial construction company proved to be one hell of a hayride, filled with ups and downs. So many exciting building remodels, interesting people and new, innovative industry developments came our way—it was a rewarding end for Jerry and me. We were left satisfied with the sense of a job well done.

A small retirement party was arranged for us in a friendly space alongside a microbrew. We were given excursion tickets for a going-away trip with spending money, as it was well known that our dream was to begin traveling. We had run the company for eighteen years, and now we were finished. We proudly handed over a solvent company with an excellent customer base and a stellar working crew to a much younger, capable new owner. We were pleased with our unexpected good fortune.

MEANWHILE, THE ORBS PICKED up in frequency on the camera. Not only did we see orbs, but a new development began to appear in the videos, dots. Dots were everywhere like swarms of tiny insects in the branches of the trees. We could not decide if maybe the camera was ruined. Then there would be nights when the video picture was clear of any orbs or dots. More high strangeness, I called this.

The swarms of dots covered the trees in the videos causing the trees to appear to be vibrating. And as if things could not get any stranger, the orbs were up in trees *with* the dots. Soon after, what looked like thousands and thousands of orbs were flowing out from the trees at a terrific rate, along with thousands of vibrating dots. Every morning we found the dots and orbs dominating the videos again. Occasionally, a foggy cloud moved across the field and over the cherry tree in the back field. To say we were confused would be putting it mildly. We did not know what it was we were seeing.

We never understood what triggered the camera to take these orb videos, as there were no deer, no coyotes and no wind blowing the tall blades of grass that lined up perfectly in front of the camera lens, causing the camera to trigger and begin filming. It was hard to know if the camera was still working correctly. Or were we photographing paranormal activity related to Sasquatch? Interesting question, we had no answers.

And then, to my even greater surprise, these dots began appearing in the bedroom at night. I could see them filling the space in the room and realized, "Yes, they could be seen by the naked eye. My naked eye!" It felt as though I had attracted them—as if my interest had attracted them to me. Maybe this is exactly what happened.

The dots were intense and energized. They filled the air space all over the room, vibrating. It made me very nervous, and they appeared every night, filling every nook and cranny. I really did not know what to do. Jerry could not see them. Both surprised and dismayed, once again, I felt isolated and stuck. The dots moved in waves encircling the room. Each night I kept my head beneath the covers until I fell fast asleep.

Nevertheless, the fun continued with the camera every morning until November, after our retirement party. One evening we were having a dinner party with friends. After dinner, we built a campfire in the backyard, and in the chilly air, we stood around the fire while the sky gently drizzled. We were having the time of our lives with everything to look forward to in retirement. We had worked hard and now were excited about our future.

The following morning, we picked up the memory card from the camera and got our mugs of tea to watch the nightly events beyond the fence. The first thing we noticed was that we could hear our voices. The trail camera recorded our voices while talking with our friends at the campfire. We could be heard faintly. The lively campfire could be heard crackling and popping.

Next, I realized there were orbs in the video. "This early in the evening?" I wondered. They were usually recorded during the early morning hours according to the time noted by the camera. Also, the orbs did not look the same. They were not moving in their usual pattern. Instead, they were solid white, not translucent like the orbs we typically saw on film. They were pure white and moved purposefully. There was no wind that night, only a gentle sprinkling of rain.

As I said, these orbs were solid light, not translucent. They were doing several new and unusual things we had never seen before in any of the videos. They could flatten out like a pancake while moving, bend at a 45° angle and turn to move in a new direction. These orbs had a mind of their own and were traveling in all directions, up and down, side to side, or they remained suspended and still in mid-air.

At the same time, impressive broad beams of light were raining down ferociously in blinding streaks. The light beams poured down all over the fields like lightning strikes—except they were utterly silent. I turned up the volume but could not hear any rain. The audio on our camera did not pick up even the faintest sound of raindrops or anything from these light beams. I surmised; the streaks of light were not rain.

Near the end of the footage, an explosion of light that appeared like an octopus, arms going out in different directions, ended our video camera. Something had come right up to our camera and overpowered it. The camera recorded its very last video that night. The trail camera no longer worked.

I could not understand what we had filmed and wondered if

this was done by Sasquatch. Maybe Sasquatch deliberately put an end to that camera? During my early period of Sasquatch research, I read several accounts where Sasquatch had blown out the electronics of various pieces of equipment. I was curious if any of the articles I had read were true.

I tended to give Sasquatch the benefit of the doubt. I understood they had very powerful energy—that had come to be one of the most important truths I learned about them. They lived here with us, but they lived in another world, one in which we are neither acquainted nor familiar.

Sometime later, while checking in with the telepathic communicator, I learned during that evening at the campfire with our friends that the Sasquatch People were giving me a big goodbye send-off. They were saying goodbye. Each November, they left for the winter and headed to a snowy area up north where they spent their winters. I suspected their goodbye send-off is what blew out the camera... It was a spectacular show and worth the ruination of the camera.

Realizing the Sasquatch People were outdoors with us that night at the campfire and giving me a personal goodbye meant a great deal to me. By now, the Sasquatch and I were developing a trusting relationship. Interestingly, I also learned that the Sasquatch did not mind the trail camera either.

Eagerly, I anticipated their return in mid-spring. I was enjoying my whole experience with them and was honored to feel part of their community. I was having an amazing experience with so much to reflect upon...

Chapter Twelve

A Life-Changing Year

TWO WEEKS AFTER THE retirement party, Jerry had his yearly physical. After a routine medical procedure, it was revealed that he had esophageal cancer. We were floored. His newly formed team of oncology doctors outlined the medical procedures ahead of him: chemotherapy, radiation therapy and major cancer surgery. This would be followed by tube feeding for three to four months. The surgery was quickly scheduled for May that next spring. The good news was that the cancer had not spread.

January through February, in ice-cold weather, I attended the cancer center four days a week with Jerry. I sat in on every radiation/chemo treatment and every doctor visit to learn everything I could. I needed to be there for Jerry to help him get through this ordeal in the best way possible. He was losing lots of weight from the radiation treatments. I became his full-time caregiver and support person.

We were both stressed by the sudden news of cancer but were

grateful it had been caught in time and had not spread. I was determined to fight with every inch of my willpower to do everything possible for Jerry and his health. I maintained a mindset that we have a golden future together. I did not allow myself to imagine any other future; it was golden, period.

LATER THAT WINTER, THE Coronavirus pandemic entered the picture. While listening to the news one evening, we learned that a highly contagious disease was spreading rapidly from country to country. By February, we wore face masks to keep our noses and mouth covered in public. Since cancer treatment destroys the body's natural immunity, Jerry and I remained isolated at home. It was essential neither of us became infected. I needed to be vigilant and protect Jerry from the virus. He was at high risk for infection and would not likely survive this virus. The freedoms with which we were so accustomed came to an end—and for how long, no one knew.

I did not allow Jerry to go out except for doctor visits. We could no longer gather indoors with family and friends. I was extra cautious while in public and wore a mask. It was unknown how the virus spread. The Center for Disease Control (CDC) was desperately scrambling for answers. Hand sanitizer became a big seller in supermarkets. Grocery store shelves stayed empty of items like sanitizer wiping pads, hand sanitizer, Clorox, rubbing alcohol, etc. Strangely, toilet paper shelves remained empty for weeks. Weekly shopping trips included searching from one store to the next, looking for a package of toilet paper to buy. These were troubling times. No one knew what the future would hold or if there was a future. Reports from the experts from the CDC dominated the news every night.

Self-isolating went okay for Jerry and me. We had sold our company, were retired and had each other to rely upon. Like most everyone, we watched the news, listened to all the CDC recommendations and followed their guidelines hoping to stay healthy and safe. We did not know if we would be okay; no one knew. No one had any idea how this pandemic would play out or just how many people would lose their lives. The evening news was filled with reported death tolls in the hundreds of thousands. There was unprecedented overcrowding in hospitals with COVID-infected patients. This became the new norm all around the United States and Europe.

WHEN SPRING ARRIVED, TO distract ourselves from the pandemic, we watched for the wild plum trees to blossom, the first native flowers to bloom each year. The days were growing longer and warmer. Soon it would be time to plant a garden. It was so important to continue doing the things we enjoyed. We needed to maintain a sense of balance and not allow our current circumstances to take over our lives. It was not easy, but we plugged along day by day.

I purchased the usual seeds, hoping we would enjoy watching them grow and eating the fresh vegetables. I planned to sow beans, cucumbers, cherry tomatoes, beets and especially lettuce. I was uncomfortable buying lettuce at the store because it was unknown how COVID-19 spread. Lettuce heads were generally stacked without packaging on open-air shelves in the grocery stores, which seemed unsafe with the rapidly spreading virus on the rampage. So, I bought my own lettuce seeds for now. One day I found a salad dressing recipe that sounded good, so I tucked it away in my brain with the plan that we would enjoy salads from the garden. It gave me something to look forward to and helped keep my spirits up.

Between COVID-19 and Jerry's cancer treatments, a gray cloud of stress blanketed the mood of our household. As if that was not enough, another situation started to brew that did not align with the excitement of spring. Feller was beginning to decline. This July, he would be 14 years old and was starting to show noticeable signs of weakness. He was becoming feeble. His powerful face and demeanor changed dramatically. He looked confused and skittish. He became thin, and he wandered all over the yard for hours. It was a blessing he did not go beyond the fence, as I worried about his condition with coyotes as neighbors. It was unbearable to watch. My sadness and concern doubled.

Feller was my "baby." We were close, as close as a cat and a human can bond. We always knew what each other was feeling. Now, I could see by his behavior that he was confused and his thinking was not quite right. But I could do nothing for him except keep him safe and monitor his health. I was not ready for his end to be near, but is anyone ever ready in this kind of situation? Some nights, I cried myself to sleep. At this point, there seemed to be too much going on.

MAY ARRIVED, AND SO did Jerry's surgery. We set out on our long journey to the hospital a day early with plans to spend the night in a nearby hotel. When we reached Seattle, the streets were empty of traffic. There were no moving vehicles on any of the roads. The hospital parking lot was empty. Jay Inslee, the Governor of Washington, mandated we self-isolate, work and stay at home if possible. It was the new sign of the times. Seattle was a ghost town. No one was driving or walking anywhere. Not a soul could be seen. In my lifetime, I had never seen Seattle so quiet. Everything was shut down for COVID.

That day seemed to take forever to pass, but we did not mind. We took each moment as if it was our very last together. We wanted these few hours before Jerry's surgery to go on forever in the event they were the last ones we would ever spend together...

The next morning, I gathered our overnight bags and got

ready to go. It was time to check in for surgery. We packed up the car and walked over to the entrance of hospital admissions. Due to COVID-19 protocol, I was not allowed inside the building, so I watched Jerry pass through the automatic sliding doors. As the doors shut, he disappeared; I could no longer see him. He had entered the unknown and was swallowed up and gone from my sight, out of my reach and out of range of my willpower fighting for his golden future. Now, I had to rely on faith for the best outcome for Jerry. The faith thing was never easy for me.

It all sank in as I headed back to the empty freeway for the long drive home. I was leaving Jerry behind for a complicated and dangerous surgery that would hopefully save his life. Silently, I allowed tears to roll down my cheeks.

After I got home, I wound up having to make some arrangements at our bank. I thought I had lost our checkbook near the hospital, so I took all the necessary steps to close that account and get set up with a new one. COVID-19 protocol was everywhere, even at local banks. At that time, our bank recommended that their customers remain inside their cars in the parking lot. The tellers came directly to car windows to conduct transactions. The teller and I set everything up and in place for a new checking account. After finishing our business together in the parking lot, I took one deep breath and left for home. To say I was physically and emotionally wiped out would be a gross understatement. That day my plate was really full.

While driving, a tire went flat. I pulled off the road and parked along the side next to a dog park. I called for tow truck assistance to come and change my flat tire. As I waited for the tow truck, a call came on my cell phone. It was from the surgeon who enthusiastically told me that Jerry's surgery was over and was a success. He told me Jerry was doing very well, and I could call him at 5 PM that evening to talk with him. It was the best news I could ever have received. Eventually, the towing representative arrived and changed my flat. I did not care how long it took; I was so relieved. As I drove home, I said over and over in my mind, "Thank you."

Jerry would be in the hospital for four days. Every day I called him, and we talked like long-lost friends. I could hear in his voice that he was extremely weak and in a great deal of pain. He had a feeding tube and explained I would learn from the nurse how to change an empty bag of food for a full one. Jerry would be on feeding bags for a while. Even though he was in a lot of pain, he talked with me daily. I missed him and wanted him to come home.

The hospital kept Jerry for two extra days. I was getting impatient for him to return home and was relieved when I could finally pick him up at the hospital. I prepared the bedroom for him with a place for the feeding tube stand. I piled lots of pillows on the bed to keep him well-propped up at a 25-degree angle. He would need to sleep propped up for the rest of his life.

Everything went smooth as silk. Jerry was home, and we slipped into an unwavering routine. I helped him with his post-surgery maintenance. He received many telephone calls from his hospital medical team checking on him and his progress. I appreciated this, as we were on a learning curve with his new medical needs. We were used to Jerry being strong with endless energy from his construction work history. This was a new reality, and we both needed time to adjust.

THINGS WERE GOING AS well as could be expected; we seemed to be making out okay. Then one day, Fusty started to have some problems of his own—he was having trouble breathing. During the visit to the veterinarian, we were told he might have a grass spur lodged in his sinuses. It was springtime, and the surrounding hay fields offered numerous opportunities for grass seeds to get lodged into the nostrils of small animals. Fusty's breathing was loud. He was struggling to get the air up through his nose. However, Fusty was in the prime of his life, and I was confident that the veterinarian would have him back on track in no time.

I kept a close watch on Jerry and both cats. I was busy and had a lot of issues to keep track of, plus I had to keep moving forward with a positive spin. I spent any extra time I had cleaning up all the flower beds; I was so busy and behind in taking care of them. They needed their winter accumulation of leaves and sticks raked and cleared away. Eventually, I planted the vegetable gardens, fertilized and got everything ready to grow. Now I could focus on my family, my family of four...

EACH NIGHT, I WAS getting lots of visits from the Sasquatch People. I sensed they were well aware of our situation and were concerned. They showed me new and different things using their energy. Around four in the morning, I would be awakened by a wall full of faces. Always, I waved my hand and smiled. There were Sasquatch children, who were much smaller and located down along the lower section of the wall near the bed. The tall adults towered up onto the ceiling. Their faces were large and facing downward at me lying in bed. I saw them there every night. If I did not wake up, they woke me. They wanted me to know they were with me and that I was not alone. I could feel the genuine caring and concern from the Sasquatch. I knew they wanted me to know they were helping and supporting all of us, cats included.

Early one morning, I woke to see a wall full of children; their small faces were scattered over the wall. I smiled and began waving at them and could see energy extending out from the wall, which I took for their arms waving back. It took some time before they learned to wave, but eventually, they all learned to wave. At first, their hands and arms looked blurry. Over time I could see the outlines of their hands and arms within the blurry energy.

They sometimes waved their hands in an up-and-down motion and changed direction and waved back and forth from side to side. I felt they were testing me to see if I could see them. I was very aware of my interactions with the children. I changed the direction of my hand each time I saw their hand change, waving to show them that, yes, I could see them fine.

There was one tiny Sasquatch child, one of the cutest I had ever seen, waving at me. He was so excited, and when I smiled and waved back, his eyes jiggled back and forth very excitedly. I was startled by the speed with which his eyes were vibrating. I hoped the child was alright. Then I noticed the same expression on another small child. His eyes were specks of light jiggling back and forth just as rapidly as the first child's. I was delighted. They were too adorable for words. To me, these people were real, and they had real lives. These youngsters were excited to connect with me. I was quite moved.

Next, I decided to direct my focus to the larger children. I had such a full heart from this experience I did not want it to end. I noticed one older youngster, around ten or eleven years old. I raised my hand in a high-five position near where I saw him/her on the wall. I wanted to show respect and see if I would get a response. To my utter astonishment, an arm surrounded by blurred light poked out from the wall. Then, the outline of a child-sized hand reached out toward mine. We did a high-five, and when our hands met, I could feel the energy from the hand of this child. It was warm, like mine! Once again, I was stunned. How was this possible that the hand was warm?

THE SUN ROSE AND set every day. No matter what was happening, life went on with all its twists and turns. One morning I woke up to find Fusty breathing louder and more labored. I took him back to the veterinarian, who kept him for a few days. After testing him for breathing problems related to felines, he was given a prescription for medicine. He was sent home with nose drops and two different medications in the form of pills. This was a nightmare for me, as I was clumsy at dispensing medicine to cats. Fusty picked up on my discomfort and outfoxed me when it came time for medication. It was a struggle, but I did my best and closely monitored his condition.

A good, steady routine kept us going. Now that Jerry was past all the cancer treatments and surgery, we could focus on recovery. After everything Jerry had been through over the last five months, this seemed simple in comparison. We met with a dietician and began organizing Jerry's healthy diet plan. He was ready now to regain his usual robust health.

For the next few days, while I watered the garden beds, Jerry and I noticed smoke in the air. The evening news reported burning homes, forests and fields in California. They were having an early, record-breaking, devastating fire season. The smoke came and went. Sometimes it was intense and made me cough. Other times, it accumulated high in the sky, blocking the sun. I had never seen anything like it before in the history of summertime wildfires. I was developing a nagging sore throat and mild headache. Fortunately, Jerry was not affected by the smoke.

One afternoon, two men who had worked with our construction crew heard the news about Jerry and the cancer. They stopped by our house after work and offered to mow our lawns for us. Arrangements were made, and after that, the two men worked together mowing our front and back lawns each week. They were happy to check in and see Jerry. They had been part of our crew for a long time and had worked with him for many years.

Meanwhile, the smoke became denser and nearly unbearable. On the evening news, we learned Canada's fire season had begun, and the air was filled with twice as much smoke. Between smoke billowing in from California and blowing down in thick waves from Canada, the sky became grayish. The sun disappeared. Jerry researched air cleaners for our house and ordered a good one. When it arrived, he installed it beside the lowboy chair where Fusty slept.

Overly taxed with concern for my family, I became distracted and forgot about the Sasquatch people, although I could plainly see they were with me all the time. I could feel them nearby, checking in with me during the day. I could feel they were fully aware of our situation and were showing me love and support. At bedtime, I stopped my usual looking for them on the wall and ceiling—I was just trying to get by, day by day, hour by hour, moment by moment. It was the best I could do. I was saddened for Jerry, my cats and all the people, animals, forests and lands terrorized by the wildfires. My heavy heart felt like a one-ton boulder sagging down into the pit of my stomach day after day.

Along with everything else, I was having problems with my vision. My surgery eye simply could not see clearly. The world was a big blur whenever I tested the vision in that eye. One eye could see; one could not. The lopsided vision affected my balance and depth perception. This made driving difficult. I stuck to the back roads and avoided the freeway. I began having a constant headache from eye strain, which often turned into an ocular migraine. My surgery eye was under so much pressure.

Finally, I just could not take it any longer. Having hit a breaking point with headaches and annoying eye strain, I quietly asked the Sasquatch People one night at bedtime for help with my surgery eye. I could see from all the dots and moving clouds that the Sasquatch were present. I asked for my eye to be healed and for clear vision once again. The peripheral vision in my surgery eye was especially troublesome. Maybe wearing an eye patch over it would help ease the strain the blurry vision created for my good eye. My good eye had excellent, clear vision but was constantly strained by the blurred vision of the other eye. I knew something needed to change.

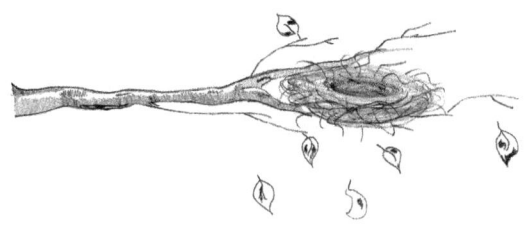

Chapter Thirteen

The End of an Era

I WAS BUSY KEEPING UP with the changing needs of my family. Grayish smoke blocked the sunlight, slightly cooling the Earth, even though it was mid-July. The smoke continuously filled the sky and became more toxic each day.

I found myself avoiding my patio of sunflowers, the place where I regularly rested and hit my reset button. This was where I self-preserved my soul and well-being. Carefully monitoring Fusty, I noted he seemed to be doing well in spite of all the smoke and was hanging in there nicely. "He's doing okay," I told myself. "These fires will eventually burn out. Fusty is going to be alright."

The CDC still had not established how COVID-19 spread, and it was spreading rapidly. One evening Jerry and I watched as the news reported that wild zoo animals in the United States were testing positive for COVID infections, animals such as hyenas and hippopotamus. So little was known about the Corona Virus, especially how it spread. Hospitals were overflowing, mortuaries were overflowing. I wondered, would this ever end?

By mid-July, the smoke let up. With the air slightly cleaner, we held a family visit. We held our visit outdoors in keeping with COVID-19 protocol. We were still not allowed to have family or friends inside our homes, so we decided moving the visit outdoors was alright. We built a warm campfire in the brick fire pit.

Jerry was on the feeding tube only part-time now. I started pureeing healthy meals for him in a food processor to supplement his daily intake of food from the feeding bags. Now, he was at a point where he could eat foods that were soft or watered-down. It was a welcome change, and he was able to eat the hot soup I made for the family gathering. We sat around the campfire eating the hot meal. The air was chilly and slightly windy, but I was so pleased to be able to see my family. They were surprised at how much smoke was in the air and did not realize how bad it had gotten. The reality of the smoke was startling for them to experience first-hand. I was happy to see everyone and grateful for the wind that day. It would serve a dual purpose and blow the smoke and potential COVID-19 germs away from us. The hot soup warmed and gave us the strength to be outdoors. We all wore our face masks when we were not eating.

Meanwhile, as we relaxed around the campfire and stretched our feet towards its warmth, Feller came to join us. He knew our extended family members well and was always happy to visit them. Everyone petted him appreciatively, talking to him like an old but not forgotten friend. Feller wanted to warm up, just like the rest of us and was trying to settle in near the fire. He was too close, and everyone became uncomfortable and noticed he was unsafe. Quickly, he was moved back safely away from the fire. He was not his usual self and had increasingly lost awareness of his surroundings. Lately, he seemed to be in a dream state. My family asked questions about Feller, and with a heart sinking like a ship lost at sea, I answered, "He is not himself anymore and is going on age 14 in one more week." My heart sank, as I could not bear it.

JUST A FEW DAYS before Feller's 14th birthday, he passed away. It took us both by surprise, although it should not have under the circumstances. Jerry was getting back his strength and could dig a hole in the backyard where Feller would be buried. Feller spent his entire life with us in this backyard and in the fields beyond the fence. These were his great hunting grounds. Our backyard was a cat paradise in many ways. Feller had the best life in the best environment with a devoted, loving family. He led a wonderful life.

We buried Feller at the bottom of the hill next to my gardens. With great care, I nestled his body into the bottom of the hole, petting him and repeatedly saying, "Goodbye, my sweet baby. Goodbye." Jerry carefully filled the hole.

THAT NIGHT I COULD plainly see the Sasquatch People all over the bedroom, letting me know they were there. Not only did I see their shadowy movements, but they also made light flashes to get my attention. They wanted me to know they were fully aware of my loss and pain and that they supported me. They were trying extra hard to get my attention. I folded my hands over my chest as I tried to rest, and I could see round lights all over my hands, blinking and moving, signaling me, trying to comfort me in my grief.

I was inconsolable. Sasquatch tried and tried to get my attention. I drifted off to sleep and wondered if, when I awoke, maybe this would be just a bad dream. Feller was always here with us, always. Now he was gone. It was unimaginable. He must *still* be here. "He can't really be gone, can he?" We were a family of four. Now, we are three. Nothing, nothing could change that.

Two days later, while resting in bed one night, I looked up

and could see the Sasquatch People on the wall, just how they presented themselves to me—but I could sense something different happening that night. They seemed flustered as if they had something they wanted me to know or see. I looked around and saw nothing except anxious, quickly moving light patterns on the wall.

Then suddenly, I felt the legs and feet of a cat drop right on top of my knees where I was lying in bed, struggling to rest and relax. The legs and feet of a tense cat were balancing on my knees as if it knew it was not supposed to be standing on my body. I did not allow cats to sleep on my feet, legs, or anywhere too near me. Never in my life did I believe it was a healthy practice. I always thought breathing fresh air was essential for a good night's sleep. The next instant, I could feel what unmistakably felt like a tense cat jumping off my legs. It felt like Feller. I looked up and did not see anything there.

Immediately, I suspected this was the doing of the Sasquatch People, trying to show me Feller was not gone. I sensed they could see him in his after-death state and brought him to me. Since I could not see him, they gently dropped him down onto my body.

I was certain Sasquatch wanted to make sure I would not miss out on Feller's visit with me and for me to realize he was not actually gone. As a fourth-dimensional species of beings, Sasquatch would not only be able to clearly see him, but they could also lift him up. Feller had passed out of his body, but maybe he had not finished his transitional end-of-life process and was still here with us temporarily in an altered form that is not physical but not wholly spirit either, an in-between state, perhaps. That was my take.

I have read accounts where pets who have passed stayed around their family for a while before leaving and entering their next world reality. Perhaps it was too soon for Feller to leave us. I would guess Feller could feel our breaking hearts... Maybe Feller could not leave yet because of me and Jerry? It seemed possible the Sasquatch could interact with Feller at this transitional point. I believe Sasquatch recognized the opportunity and took it. They wanted me to know there is never really an end.

It was a good lesson for me. I was beginning to believe that we do not actually die in the sense that we no longer exist. It must be true, then. We live on in some alternative form. Sasquatch wanted me to know that Feller was not gone; I simply could not see him. Feller was still here. Now, it would be possible for me to grieve his loss over time. At least I had a toehold in coping with his loss. Feller was not gone; he was still here. I just could not see him. Sasquatch helped me at a time I really needed it. Thank you, Sasquatch People...

CALIFORNIA WILDFIRES HAD REACHED record-breaking heights. Miles and miles of homes and acres upon acres of land were being swept up and engulfed in flames. Sadly, thousands of people were evacuated from everything they owned. At the same time, still more areas were threatened by the fast-moving inferno. People lost their homes, their animals...everything.

In many cases, there was nothing left. The smoke from the devastating fires was sent high into the atmosphere and spread great distances. For me, that summer will be remembered as the summer the sun could not shine. The sun was a helpless speck of dim light, losing the daily battle to shine through the choking, gray barrage of smoke.

Somehow, we managed day by day. I had estimated mid-September to be a logical birthdate for Fusty. Since both cats were strays, we could only estimate their actual date of birth. Fusty would be eight years old.

Now that Feller was gone, I made plans to spend even more time with Fusty. I bought him an extra-fuzzy blanket to snuggle into on the bed, plus a fuzzy-wuzzy cat bed, which I moved into the bedroom. Feller had never allowed Fusty to sleep in the room with Jerry and me. Now it was time for Fusty to have it all. I was making all kinds of plans with Fusty. Maybe we would have five or six more years together? We could have exciting, special years to still be a family. I was looking forward to completely bonding with this beautiful cat soul.

He picked right up on my intentions and played his role well. He appreciated his beds and snuggled on them often. I could brush him uninterrupted now, and he cuddled up with me on the sofa during the news every night. It became an excellent routine.

Jerry was doing well, and with Fusty by my side, everything was going to be alright. The lettuce varieties I planted grew into tender heads, and the cucumbers were sweet and crispy. One evening I picked enough vegetables and made a salad of beautiful green lettuce leaves, juicy sliced cucumbers and sweet cherry tomatoes topped off with nasturtium blossoms. I made the salad dressing recipe I had found earlier that year and made a delicious, succulent side dish. The salad was tasty and good. I added salads to our dinners from then on.

In September, the maple trees started dropping their leaves. A thick yellow carpet covered every inch of the ground in the backyard. It was stunning. The air was cold and crisp now. The tip of my nose turned red when I spent time outdoors.

Jerry was passing all his doctor visits with flying colors. His complexion was returning, as was his overall health. He had reached a point where he was ready to eat regular foods and had a wider variety of meal choices. I began preparing richer foods to help him gain back some weight. He had lost 54 pounds and looked very peaked.

It took some time and education to get up to speed on feeding a gastrectomy survivor. Their stomach winds up very small. Food needed to be packed with vitamins and minerals in each bite. It was challenging for both of us. Jerry was accustomed to having a good appetite, but things were different now. This process would take time and patience.

The wildfires were burning with a vengeance, as though they would never fizzle out. Smoke was pouring in from both the north and south. Once again, the air was thick and toxic. Soon after, one morning, I could see Fusty struggling for breath. Immediately, I took him back to the cat clinic again for what I did not realize would be the last time I would ever see him... The night before had been a bad night for Fusty. The veterinarian recommended that he be put down, saying that this was in his best interest. She explained that he had taken a turn for the worse and was suffering from brain damage due to a lack of oxygen...

COVID-19 protocol regulations allowed only animal patients inside the building. Under these unique circumstances, they graciously offered to make an exception for me to be there with Fusty at the end to say my goodbyes. I blurted out emotionally into my phone that two months ago, I had just buried my other cat, Feller. "It was too hard to see Feller's lifeless body. I just went through that. I can't see Fusty's lifeless body, too." It was too hard on me. They reassured me they would be loving and gentle. They reassured me that the entire staff would all be there with Fusty.

My world was changing at such a high speed that I could barely keep up. I waited in my car, complying with everything they asked to painlessly end the suffering of poor Fusty. At the end of Fusty's consultation, and after I made payment arrangements, I suddenly found myself choking back the tears and said, "We were a family..." My mind went blank. Somehow, I was able to drive home...

The veterinary clinic sent me several items in memory of Fusty. I was given a plaster paw print impression of his two front feet and a framed paw print picture of his two front feet in ink. I received a sympathy card in the mail containing a wonderful poem about cats and their owners. Everyone in the clinic signed the card offering sympathy for the loss of our "family member."

Jerry dug a hole at the bottom of the hill next to my garden beds, and we buried Fusty alongside Feller. These two male cats, who were like brothers, were together again. Maybe they would be together forever. I liked to think so; I needed to think so. —My beloved cats.

Jerry and I began adjusting to life without our cats. We made plans to take fun trips and worked hard, keeping our minds off the sad parts of the year. If mention of one or both cats came up, we talked it through and ended the conversation by sharing a good memory of them.

It became necessary for Jerry to sleep in something other than the bed loaded with pillows, so we bought a comfortable recliner for him. We made it into a bed, and Jerry began sleeping much better. He was regaining his energy and could take over more and more of his role and duties. He was doing very well.

We moved the bed into the spare room, and I began sleeping there. It was lonely at first, but I managed. Around two weeks or so after the passing of Fusty, I was awakened in my new bedroom during the middle of the night. It was very dark, but I could see lights flashing urgently at me from the wall. When the Sasquatch 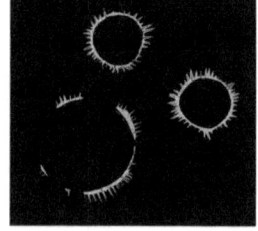 People wanted me to wake up, they sent out circular, brilliant flashes of light, bright like a strobe light. The Sasquatch children also sent me flashes of light; only theirs were half the size. I could see their bright flashes even when my eyes were shut. When I was asleep, their flashes were so bright they woke me. They were blinding, penetrating and impossible to miss. The Sasquatch were very powerful people. Their powers never ceased to amaze me.

In anticipation, I saw that the Sasquatch were here for a visit. Sasquatch faces were all over the walls and ceiling. I was pleased to see them. They were my family, my alternate family. Tonight, however, they appeared to be overly excited. They were not here to just visit, as I could see by their moving shadows. They were trying to signal something important to me.

I kept smiling and waving, and at the same time, they became more frantic. I did not understand what could be the problem. Was there something going on? All at once, a powerful sense to turn around towards the wall filled my mind. I believed the Sasquatch were sending me a "mind speak" message, a loud message sent telepathically. "Ah," I thought to myself. "This must be what the ruckus is all about. My Sasquatch friends want me to see something." By now, I was really interested in the presentations from Sasquatch. I turned towards the wall, and as I turned to look, a long, thin light caught my eye. Focusing on the thin light, I could plainly see a tail, a cat tail. A cat's tail was poking out from the wall and was hovering over my pillow. I could see the texture of fur and stripes along the tail length. I followed the tail with my eyes to the wall, where I saw a blurry, whitish light, an obscure light the same color as the tail.

I realized all at once the Sasquatch wanted me to see Fusty. Fusty was here to see me. Slowly the indistinct splotch of light became more clear, and the exact shape and details of Fusty slowly emerged. He was in a sitting position with his head turned back towards me. In this sitting position, his body was extended out beyond the wall. The wall did not exist, but the space he needed to sit and watch me—did exist. There was Fusty and no wall; however, there was space. It looked just like Fusty, alright, but he was made out of this light energy, spirit light. A large and blinding halo glowed around him, making it difficult to see his details. I could see his usual three-dimensional shape as if he were alive and in the flesh. He was looking over at me, and I could see his love for me in his expression. He seemed happy to see me and was calm and contented. He was beautiful—truly magnificent. Looking peaceful, he stayed positioned on the wall for several moments. Suddenly, he disappeared, leaving no trace that he had just been there with me. I was stunned and wondered if anyone in this world saw the kinds of things I was seeing. With a broken heart, I asked, "Fusty, why did you have to leave?"

But just as in the case with Feller, Fusty was not actually gone. He was simply somewhere else. I could plainly see that he was still here with me. He was simply in another form.

Thank you, Sasquatch People, for showing me the truth about my cats…You are changing me and my life. I am truly grateful…

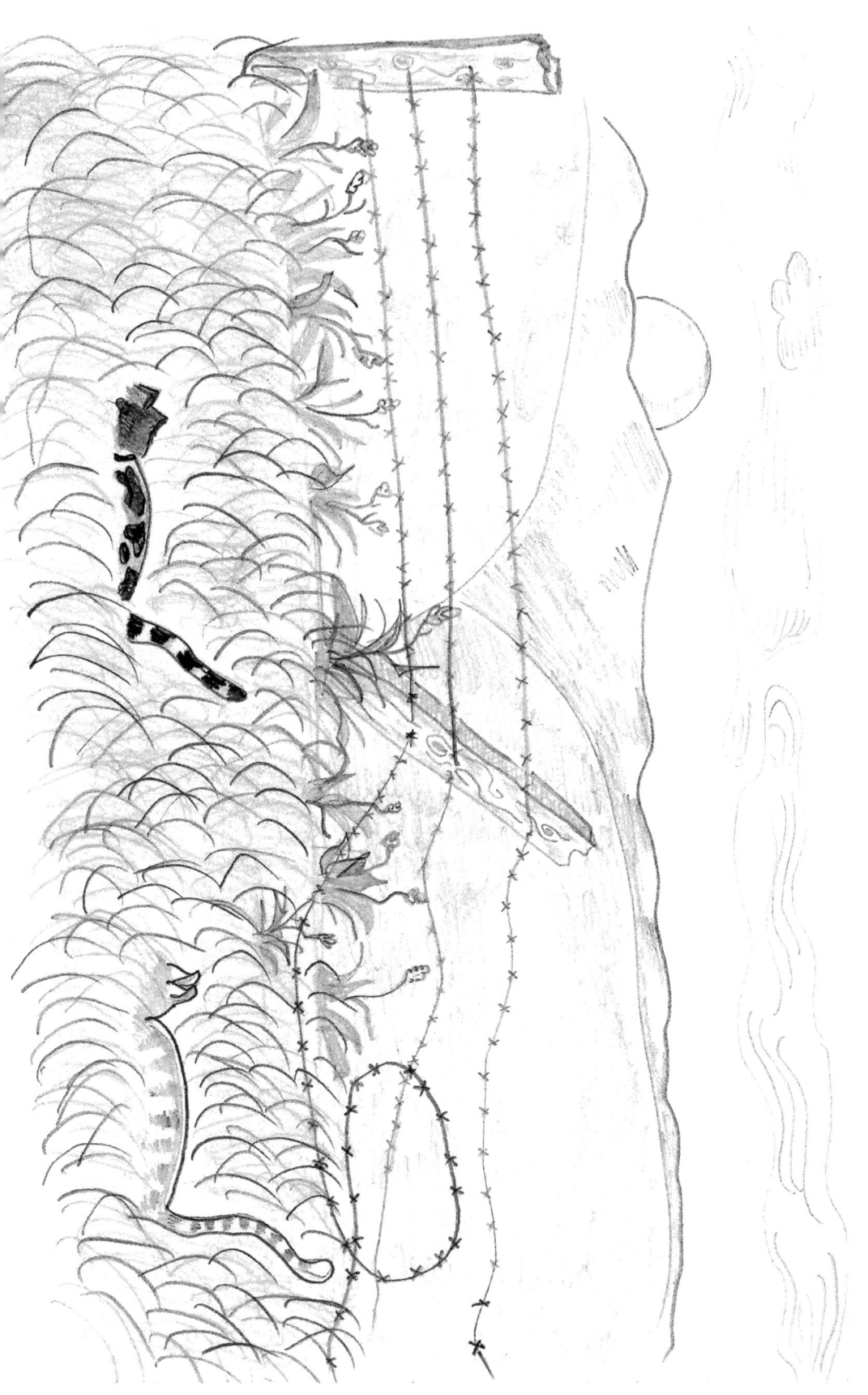

Epilogue

IT HAS BEEN DIFFICULT to say goodbye to Feller and Fusty, my baby and my prince. They were two of the most important things Jerry and I shared as a couple. We are both on our second marriage, and have two children each from a previous marriage. The cats did not represent one side of our family or the other—these cats were ours together, our family, and we loved them very much. We were a family of four...

They are buried side by side on our land, a land that sheltered them and provided them the ideal environment for a beautiful cat life. Their memory will live on as long as Jerry and I live. They are truly missed. We do not plan to take on more cats, as we have decided to travel. Maybe a trip to Europe is in our future?

After the passing of our beloved cats, we noticed other interesting and exciting changes happening in our country paradise. Birds could enter the front and backyards safely now. While the cats protected the property, I regularly chased birds and their families away for their own protection. It has been gratifying to not only allow them to nest, feed and play on our lawns, in our gardens and in our trees but to know that they can now make this their home.

We set up winter feeding stations for them when the weather turns cold. The ground usually freezes solid, and the suet blocks and birdseed mixtures keep our fine feathered friends going until mid-spring. At that time, they abandon our yard to mate and nest.

Jerry and I continue to pick up garbage along our county roads wearing our safety vests and using our handy trash grabbers. I have noticed that cleaning up litter gives me the feeling I am making a difference for the planet, no matter how small. Small or not, it is of equal importance. I also find that proactively dealing with the trash helps me relieve the stress I have associated with our confused and chaotic world. It allows me to feel like I am part of the solution. —This is indeed a good feeling.

The vision in my surgery eye is restored. One morning I woke up able to see clearly through both eyes. My eyesight is so clear that I have since been able to drive the car on the freeway and at night. Thankfully, my peripheral vision is entirely intact now, too.

I recently asked the Sasquatch People about the wild animal projection shown on the bedroom wall back during the early stages of getting acquainted. When asked if these were animals from their homeland, I was answered by another male Sasquatch elder, Thoryn. He stepped forward and told me, *"Humans have too much fear and destroy animals that are good for them."* He went on to explain the purpose of the projection was to show me animals that existed at one time on Earth but are now gone. They wanted to impress upon me that more of our animals are disappearing from existence just as these have done. The Sasquatch warns us that every animal, every plant, every river, etc., has an important purpose. *Messing with even one part weakens the whole.*

The Sasquatch People visit me every day and night. I learn new things from them, and I am advancing in my ability to see them and be with them. Also, I am getting more detailed messages from them. This has been my experience with the Sasquatch People.

I hope that you, dear reader, can find something useful here for your life. Thank you for taking the time to read my story.

Discussion

Humans are Part of the Earth, Not the Center of It

THE SASQUATCH HAVE REACHED a point where they feel it is time to jump in and help mankind. They want us to understand that they are not dangerous and want us to learn about them and their purpose. They say it is getting closer to the time to bridge the gap between themselves and human beings. They plan to live in their physical form alongside humans, as they have in the distant past. They plan to guide and help us heal our lives and the Earth.

There are several things the Sasquatch want us to know about them. First and foremost, they want us to see that they are not monsters. They do not harm or kill. They are benevolent beings of a highly evolved species of people. They are powerful—a power that can help guide and heal mankind. Their world is one of unconditional love, and they live in harmony with nature. They want to share their higher truths and teach us how to achieve our highest level of existence here on Earth. They say we can do it, especially now at this desperate time.

Sasquatch are experts on appropriate behavior. They feel each of us needs to ask ourselves, "What is important for my life?" Their encouragement directs us to turn within, alone time as we like to call it. They say we are living in an unprecedented powerful time energetically, a time of powerful energy shifts. This time of high energy is quite unique, and the opportunity to create significant changes in our lives and the world is now.

They do not want us to miss our opportunity. Now is the time. —We can heal our lives and the lives of our family and friends. Right now, we can make miracles happen.

Sasquatch explains that higher spirit beings, who possess the same powerful energy, have also been assisting us in healing and becoming more enlightened about the natural ways of coexisting on our planet—and these higher beings include Sasquatch. All higher spirit beings use an energy called love. It is the most powerful energy in the universe and can cause great energetic shifts on Earth. Love is a healing, cleansing power available for us to use to rid ourselves of negativity and, in turn, create positive outcomes within each aspect of our lives—our health and the health of our families and friends, our interpersonal relationships, our level of abundance and our need for a clean and perfectly balanced planet for the future, to name just a few. This is the shortlist. The complete list is long—very long. We must be careful and not place limitations on this list or on ourselves, as there are a lot of issues to acknowledge and resolve.

The Sasquatch urge us to open our hearts and create a wonderful world. They see us as beings who have forgotten how powerful we indeed are. We have allowed superficial ideals and outside influences to tell us who we are, how we should live, etc. Thus, we have inadvertently blocked our own natural knowingness and flow. We have relinquished our unique personal power in favor of outdated, manmade paradigms that tell us how to live by following ideals that are thin and weak. These paradigms are supported only because we humans support them. We believe them to be the true, end-all ideology we must follow and never question. The minute we quit accepting will be the end for them. They will deflate and become unnoticeable. They will take on the same form as the historic myths we read about in history. They will be nostalgic and unrelated to how the world works, like all the rest of the world myths in our literature. Our world is moving into a reality that vibrates at a much higher rate and speed. We will see remarkable changes; we will make extraordinary changes.

Each one of us possesses our own unique inner wisdom and our own innermost truth. We need to remember how to trust ourselves. Sasquatch wants us to remember who we are and what we are capable of. They say we can and will restore humanity and the Earth. They have confidence in us, and now we need to have that same confidence in ourselves.

Sasquatch said, "Many humans struggle with loneliness and disconnection from others. They resist the changes needed to come into this new energy and have a happy, free life. They are scared and need love. They are good people but are struggling." This is the problem, as Sasquatch sees it.

When asked about the pandemic, Sasquatch answered that COVID is an opportunity for humanity to look inward and learn to be kind, courteous and loving towards one another. They also see a need for humankind to adopt the kind of protective love that parents have for their children and to extend this loving care to others around them who are in need. We are urged to extend ourselves beyond our current social boundaries and help uplift and support one another, especially those in desperate need. We need to be like parents and assist those suffering the most to help them elevate their lives. Sasquatch wants us to support each other in becoming happy. This is what the Sasquatch strongly recommends.

Sasquatch says we humans are not getting the point about being kind, loving and considerate to one another. "The pandemic will be around for a long time," answered Mannie after I asked him, "Will it end sometime soon?" "They are not getting it," said Mannie. "They're still not getting it." Until enough of us understand the importance of changing our behaviors toward one another, diseases and pandemics will probably be our reality for a long time to come.

However, after enough of us have raised our frequency and can lead our life harmonizing with others and nature, we will all be lifted out of the clutches of the negative energy we have created over years and years. Those resisting will automatically be lifted, including the ones that cannot help themselves or just do not want to. The collective power that will come from human beings who have raised their frequency will overpower the negative energy from the opposing population that does not want things to change. Their energy will rise too. The Sasquatch commented that the opposing part of the human population is weakening. Sasquatch said, "Eventually, they will have little power. They will still be there, but they will be small. No one will listen."

Higher frequencies released by advanced spirits are proving more effective when coming through humans already healing themselves and/or are in the healing process. The high energy released by these spirit beings becomes magnified through these individuals in the healing process. In turn, the amplified energy expands and reaches many more people worldwide. This is an exciting and unexpected outcome from combining the two energies. This is speeding up the healing of the Earth. The positive reaction made by the two intense energies was a pleasant, unexpected surprise. The Sasquatch were all very pleased.

The Sasquatch continued directing attention toward how poorly humans treat each other, especially during wars and all the killing. They made this a vital point: "Killing has to stop now." In their world, killing does not exist. The Sasquatch are always courteous, kind, and loving to one another. They encourage us to upgrade our skills in our interpersonal relationships. They believe we must learn to be good to one another. Sasquatch says we will make the most significant difference on Earth when we upgrade our interpersonal relations. Herein lies the biggest key for the fastest changes.

The timing of the Sasquatch messages is just about right. Humanity appears to be lost, and people are looking for a more profound truth. We need a higher paradigm that is more humanistic to follow, one which embodies higher truths, higher values, authentic purpose and connection to others and to life. Not all, but many of us have reached our saturation point, endlessly owing our lives to a two-dimensional, greed-based corporate job to the point it seems our life is no longer our own. Joylessly, many of us plod along day after day—because we must, not because we are excited to see what each glorious new day will bring. —We are burning out because we live against life and nature.

The hardcore stress from ever-present climate change, the unending pandemic, chronic homelessness and drug addiction, the possibility of nuclear war, and so forth has profoundly affected the quality of life for our entire world. Many of us feel desperate and have sent our antennae high into the stratosphere, searching for answers, reasons, purpose, justice, balance, hope, connection, belonging, and love—just something we can grasp and hold onto during these tumultuous and uncertain times.

These are a few of the reasons why the Sasquatch People see the need for us to go within, find our truth, and become our true selves. This may be the right time for Sasquatch to help us achieve this balance within ourselves and the world. Sasquatch also stresses the need for humankind to understand how we work, how nature works, and how the two work together. So many of us have lost our balance and lost ourselves long, long ago.

As I continued learning from Sasquatch, I slowly began understanding a portion of the whole picture. I suggested writing a book about the truth of the Sasquatch and their message to humanity. They were both pleased and excited. They want their love and peaceful living messages to be available for everyone. They have confidence that we are evolving and becoming the enlightened beings we once were in the past.

Sasquatch can be contacted by humans through the heart. When your heart truly yearns to connect with them, they will come to you without fail. They hear you through your heart. All communication is made through a loving heart. Love is a powerful and specific energy we need to use to connect with Sasquatch People.

You can speak to Sasquatch with your heart at any time. They will hear you and answer you in a unique way that matches who you are. They seem to understand us better than we do. It is easy to reach them. If you are interested, simply be sincere, and you will contact them. Be aware that you may find yourself amid "high strangeness." At this time, you would know that you have made a connection to Sasquatch. They will have your very best interests in mind. —You will indeed be very fortunate!

For the most part, Sasquatch are invisible. They live in an alternate dimension known as the fourth dimension. They can see us from their alternate dimension, as only a thin wall of energy called the "veil" separates our world from theirs. Sasquatch People can pop in and out between these two dimensions. They can also rise up into the fifth dimension. Often, they are referred to as interdimensional beings by Sasquatch experts and experiencers, meaning they exist in more than one dimension.

Due to their interdimensional existence, they can easily stay out of sight; however, we can hear them and see all kinds of evidence left by them. Sometimes they materialize into our third-dimensional reality to experience nature and its wonders, such as forests, weather, berries, fruits, etc. Occasionally, they are sighted by people, but only because they have allowed themselves to be seen. Rarely are they ever caught off guard. They are very aware when humans are present.

The Sasquatch dwell in heavily forested areas and can travel far from their home turf. While traveling, they move in their energetic form. They can move from one location to another through trees. This mode of travel is referred to as teleporting. This sounded incredible to me until, one day, I could see their energy move in and out of trees. I do not expect anyone to believe me here. I can only believe it myself because I have witnessed it many, many times.

There are a lot of misrepresentations surrounding the mysterious and controversial Sasquatch, partially because there is no scientific way to verify their existence. However, what does it matter if we ever scientifically prove facts about Sasquatch? Whether we have evidence that qualifies under scientific methods will not make any difference to our world. They are not a threat; they never have been and never will be. Never. After all, they have not tried to take over the world. If they were as powerful and evil as is suggested by some sources, a takeover would have happened by now.

One thing I understand about Sasquatch is that they are peaceful. It is not in their nature to have an ambition such as power.

They see the world as an entity with several essential components making up the whole. They will never deviate from the piece of life to which they belong.

I HAVE LEARNED TO see Sasquatch in their energetic form. It took a few years and a lot of practice—they provided me with daily opportunities. My home is not in a wilderness setting; therefore, I experience Sasquatch while they are in their energetic form.

They travel into my home often, and I regularly see their shimmer of energy. Their shimmer looks like the watery surface of a pond or lake, only this surface is upright; it is vertical and not horizontal. Also, I usually hear odd sounds when they are around. Often, I have listened to them sit down noisily in a living room chair. One Sasquatch sat right down on the leather armchair in the living room. The sound of impact was loud and impossible to miss. Glancing over at the chair, I could see Sasquatch energy shimmering all the way up to the ceiling.

Although there are families of Sasquatch People living in and around this area, the family of Sasquatch with whom I have a connection does not actually live here. Since they visit me from somewhere else, I will never hear them vocalize, see their footprints, etc., as they are here as energy and not physical, not materialized.

I may never see the impressive territory markers they build using yanked-out trees intricately and tightly woven together like the ones pictured on legitimate Sasquatch websites. The remarkable tree structures are found deep in the forests. They are constructed for the purpose of staking out territory.

Too, I will not discover their footprints on a forest path or in the snow because they do not materialize into physical form this far away from their home. This Sasquatch family leaves my area in November and returns early in March. Once, I asked Sasquatch why they go in November and return in the spring. Their answer was, "We like snow." I do not know where home is for them. When I asked them, "Where is your home?" Their answer was, "To the east."

Lately, they have been selecting humans they feel will believe the "truth of them." They are on the lookout for candidates with whom to develop a connection. They want to teach more human beings about them as a species of people while, at the same time, guiding us toward our better good. I do not know all the details about their human choice selections. I was selected because I was at a crossroads in my life. Deep inside, I felt that getting closer to nature was the most important thing I could do for my well-being. I was open, and sensing the truth of them was not hard. Deep inside, I felt they had an answer and a way out of the critical problems we face in our world today. We are caught in what appears to be a too-little, too-late stage of global warming. But Sasquatch believes there is still time to turn things around. Sasquatch has answers. They are waiting in the wings, ready to help us learn.

Over time, I have been exposed to other Sasquatch groups living in North America. Each of these communities has a portion of nature to protect and guard as their life purpose. Some groups call themselves People of the Forest. Others call themselves River People.

The Sasquatch in my community—and all Sasquatch for that matter—focus on behavior. For the most part, I am discovering that my community of Sasquatch is concerned about the quality of our state of being and how we mistreat each other poorly. They want us to upgrade our values, ethics and morals. They want to show us their view of reality, which coincides in complete harmony with the cycles of the Earth. They live in perfect synchronicity with the world and want to teach us how to live this way. Sounds good to me—what do we have to lose?

I have learned that the Sasquatch love and care about us unconditionally. It is their oneness with nature that makes them unconditionally loving. They have watched many of us live out our lives, coming and going through our natural life cycles of birth and death. Humans come and go quickly compared to Sasquatch. At one point during my research, I ran across a source I believed legitimate, which talked about Sasquatch having a life span of over 1,000 years.

Whether this is true or not, I would not know. Other sources that I have read reveal different answers. But what does it matter? I asked Sasquatch, "How long do you live?" Their response was, "Long." Sasquatch does not recognize nor rely on linear, sequential timelines. From what I understand, space and time do not exist in the dimension where they live. That is my take on it anyway, unscientific, not even mathematical. It just does not seem to matter.

Since they live much longer lives than humans, they have had the opportunity to observe our evolution as a species. Now they want to step into view and be part of everyday life alongside us. They see us as their younger brothers and sisters and feel a responsibility to help us get through this troubling time. They understand what we are going through and are sad we are suffering.

We are expiring on the Earth, and the Earth is expiring on us. Sasquatch are not affected by the same changes in the world that we are experiencing. They can always see us from their fourth-dimensional plane. In various sources, I have read that from their fourth-dimensional point of view, it is like they are in the same house with us, only they are in a different room.

Near the end of my experience writing this story, I received some more critical messages from Mannie about how human beings have been living and how they use the planet with little to no regard. Sasquatch strongly feels we are living against nature.

Mannie says, "Humans are ridding the Earth of themselves by how they live. *They are part of the Earth, not the center of it.*" He further states, "The Earth will heal itself completely if we allow it to. The Earth will heal itself completely when we are all gone. Getting rid of humanity will be like a great detox for the Earth." This was startling to hear, but it is true. He was only speaking the truth.

Mannie wants us to fully understand that the trees, weather, uncultivated land, oceans, lakes and rivers are essential components that make up the delicate framework that keeps the cycles of the Earth healthy and going strong. Not only do human beings interfere with a portion of these important, critical pieces of the framework, but they also interfere with all of them. We do not seem to believe we are making grave judgment errors when we build a dam across a river or produce toxic poisons, etc.

Suppose we want to continue existing here on Earth. If so, we must allow each component of Earth's framework to be healthy and function properly. This is how life on Earth sustains itself; it is through each of these functions that combine and work together in cooperation and which rely on each other as both a part and as a whole—the rivers, forests, uncultivated land and so forth… There is no other way out of this reality. We have to face it now and make new plans for how to live.

Dreamtime

DREAMTIME IS A SPECIFIC mental state. It is a state of being where humans can connect with Sasquatch. Dreamtime is both a time and a space where our brains have slowed down enough that we can be approached by Sasquatch. They can work with us and visit with us during dreamtime. We can have experiences and can talk with very genuine beings. I have come away from dreamtime refreshed, healed, and more of who I truly am. The experiences are rewarding in terms of growth and development as a human being. I do mention this a lot, "growth and development." It is the most important thing each one of us human beings can accomplish in our lifetime. The Sasquatch are very specialized in this arena and are ready to help us immediately.

During my dreamtime experiences, my thoughts are lucid, and I experience a place that feels very real with real people. While in this state, I can talk with Sasquatch, and I can see them. It seems like a dream, a dream that is on steroids. The experience is different from any experience I have had to date. All my memories of interacting with Sasquatch during dreamtime are good.

I look forward to the next experience with Sasquatch and enjoy being around them, as they are nonjudgmental and unconditionally loving. The Sasquatch are teachers who guide us toward our better good. They are much more advanced than humans, and their powers are extraordinary.

My first experience in dreamtime was like taking a trip somewhere new to meet a family. I was taken to a place I had never seen before, a country or area that looked like our Earth but was different. It felt peaceful and serene. It was nighttime, as there was no sun in the sky. We were in a forest with tall trees and minimal undergrowth. We walked over trails through woods well cleared of rocks, roots or brush. It was a beautiful forest, and I could see great distances between the trunks of the trees—I could see that the forested area was vast. It felt very safe.

I was attended by two Sasquatch men who were gentle, kind and had excellent manners. They felt just like family and were my tour guides showing me around. I enjoyed their company very much and was comfortable being around these two Sasquatch, as they were courteous and considerate. Effortlessly, we traveled through the forest. I became aware that we did not need to move our feet to walk; it was optional. Letting go of the awareness to move my feet, I simply experienced what was presented to me. I sensed that this was their home, where they lived.

While moving forward on a narrow trail, we came across a large, wild cat. It was not one of the large, wild cats with which I was familiar; it was slightly larger than a bobcat but marked differently. The colors were the same, and the fur was the same, but the markings were not like those on our bobcats or any other wild cat here on Earth.

One extraordinary quality I sensed from the cat was that it was not a predator. I did not get the sense I usually get while face-to-face with a dangerous animal. Also, the cat did not appear afraid but seemed quite interested in us. His expression struck me—his eyes appeared human. It probably would have responded if I had wanted to talk with this big cat. The cat seemed to have a human conscience and behaved like it was our equal. This attitude made the cat wholly different from any wild animal I have ever encountered. During this meeting with the cat, —*I knew I was no longer in Kansas!*

The cat watched the two Sasquatch men and me as it sat between two trees in the middle of the trail. Somehow, we got past the big cat without a lick of effort and continued further down the path. The big cat did not seem the slightest bit disturbed by our presence. Most remarkable about this wild cat was its lack of fear. It never moved or changed position while resting between the two trees. It seemed curious about me. Maybe it was trying to make out what kind of creature I was? It may never have seen a human before.

This experience filled in the answer to my ever-persistent question, "Where does the Sasquatch live, and what does it look like?" The Sasquatch answered me by taking me along to see for myself. It was a generous and thoughtful gesture on their part. This was my first experience where I felt genuine trust for them.

Due to the critical circumstances facing our world, dreamtime is now reserved for healing purposes only. Much healing takes place in dreamtime, and humans must have access to this state of mind to heal, grow and develop. The Sasquatch are adept at helping humans. I know I have received a lot of benefits from their life-changing attention.

Presently, all my dreamtime visits are behavioral lessons. In one of my more recent lessons, I clearly remember a Sasquatch teacher sitting on the ground next to a man who was socially awkward and troubled. This man had received a lot of ridicule in his life and was now expecting more for some apparent problem he had just created. Usually, I would launch verbally with my judgments and opinions. This time I held back, unsure.

To my great surprise, the Sasquatch teacher began verbally lambasting the man with each of the judgments I had just been thinking. Each time a judgmental thought passed through my mind, the Sasquatch teacher criticized the man harshly, using my very words. It was startling to witness.

Stranger, yet, each time the man was scolded, the Sasquatch teacher's face grew more and more unattractive. His face seemed to be coming apart with each disparaging remark. He checked to make sure I was paying attention and swung his head back and forth a couple times for dramatic effect. It was dramatic—small bits of face flew off in different directions as he jerked his head back and forth.

I could see the teacher's eyes studying me to know whether I fully comprehended that the harsh judgments were not harming the troubled man—they were hurting the Sasquatch teacher for delivering them. The lesson continued until the Sasquatch teacher was convinced that I could understand the lesson and piece it all together. By the end of that lesson, the teacher looked like a rotting corpse. Startling as this lesson was, it was very effective.

I got it. I understood that the lesson was presented for my benefit, to teach me not to judge. Now, as a result of this new understanding, I want to practice using compassionate words to show love for the man, as well as for humankind in future experiences. The lesson was powerful. Now, my goal is to have compassion for people rather than irritation when things don't go according to plan. I have felt myself becoming more peaceful on the inside, gaining peace of mind and tranquility with the world. I hope to visit dreamtime for years to come. After each dreamtime experience, my world becomes calm and sublime. I owe the Sasquatch People much for all their healing and lifestyle guidance.

In a surprising turn of events, I am now regularly visited by other Sasquatch representatives from different family communities that live way up north where humans are rarely seen. They have heard about me from other Sasquatch People. Word seems to get around.

These new Sasquatch elders from the north have been visiting me since spring. They have been giving me the message that their community advocates—messages that will help humans restore natural law and order within themselves and nature. They hope I will also write another book and include their important messages. Sasquatch are indeed the Guardians of the Earth.

Based on my experiences with Sasquatch, I believe they are organizing at this critical time to live alongside human beings to help us restore the planet. I hope humans embrace them as I have and welcome them into their lives. They have made a tremendous difference in mine. Through my experiences with Sasquatch, I have gained in so many ways. I have been able to feel myself morphing and sculpting into my true self, a self I can be proud of.

Growth, Development and New Perspectives

IT IS TIME NOW for a word about healing trauma. Sasquatch has good news for those interested in healing their lives. After a few years of getting acquainted with Sasquatch, I realized that recovering from my past needed to be center stage for me. It was time to heal my life, and Sasquatch are expert healers. They were right there, ready to help me. There comes a time for all of us to rid ourselves of the nagging baggage of unresolved life issues that we fully expect to take to the grave. It is time to become the people we were meant to be, who we really are as spirit—a spirit in a human form filled with confidence, joy and in charge of creating positive and fulfilling lives for ourselves and others.

Healing is of paramount importance, and the time to heal was *yesterday*. Why continue to live life in a holding pattern for a better tomorrow? Or live your life, day by day, waiting for someone else to make a positive move towards a brighter future tomorrow? Why not consider that we are operating within that reality *now*? We could really benefit by shifting our perspective—right now. Why wait? During our thoughts and perceptions, it is much more powerful to have good ideas about our lives right now as we speak. What if tomorrow does not come? It would benefit us if we *expected* beautiful things in our world—a solid expectation—no ifs, ands, or buts. Also, *right now* works in sync with the vibrational shifts now present on the planet. The old way of perceiving our future: maybe tomorrow will be a better day, will get you just that, perhaps tomorrow, a holding pattern. I have been experimenting with my life by sticking "right now" into my mind. Each time I slip back into the old routine of expecting doom and gloom, I start over and stick 'right now' back into my brain. It will take practice, for sure. Changing our perspective to "right now" is a more powerful frame of reference than "hoping for a better tomorrow."

We get pretty much what it is we focus on. Sasquatch sees we have another choice. They watch us from the other side and urge us to change our focus. We have the power to choose conditions of life that are wonderful, magnificent and rewarding. They see we have lost belief in ourselves and our abilities. We are all receiving precisely what we believe, whether pleasant or otherwise. Plus, we are surrounded by deafening negativity from the media. As a gift to yourself, tune it out. At least part of the time. Many of us are struggling with negative information overload and need a break to regroup ourselves and our life.

In the beginning stages of getting to know Sasquatch, they could literally see the trauma inside my body; they could see it as energy. They decided it was time for me to get it cleared out of my life. Since then, I have been healing nightly while I sleep. If I happen to wake up, I can see the energy they use in the darkness of the bedroom. It looks gritty and sparkly everywhere. The room becomes filled with this fascinating, glittering energy as it raises my vibration.

I can feel the effects of this energy, too. Most mornings, I wake up feeling renewed. It positively affects me during my day-to-day functioning. I feel terribly lucky and want others to have this same opportunity.

At times, as part of the healing process, it is necessary to feel the pain from the original trauma. This can take a few days to process, but afterward, I feel entirely at peace with myself and the world. The work is worth it. I feel amazing and transformed when I get through each healing session.

Sometimes, there are lessons attached to the healing during dreamtime, as I discussed earlier. In the morning, after a dream-time lesson, I receive new ideas and innovative solutions to use as tools. I have many new tools and ways to handle the tricky parts of my life.

Another important message from Sasquatch is about our *over-enthusiasm for materialism* rather than *enthusiasm for spirituality*. Mannie says we need to go within ourselves and make decisions based on what is best for our overall good. Sasquatch wants us to heal by spending time alone in nature. I sense that Sasquatch believes we will be every bit as fulfilled by our spiritual experiences, and we will not need our worldly possessions the way we do now. Sasquatch suggests the spiritual realm is more fulfilling than the material world. They believe we will outgrow the need for so many material things. They wish we would try.

How are the Sasquatch People able to help us now? They possess powers as interdimensional beings that go far beyond our comprehension. Their powers are evidence of the quantum-physical field in which they live. They vibrate at a much higher frequency and at a much faster speed. Their energy is so powerful that you will feel like a great force is responding to you when they are there with you.

Sasquatch are all too aware that this present time on Earth is critical. They are keenly aware of global warming and the pandemic. They are very mindful that we need help. They see us as their younger brothers and sisters and feel a responsibility to help us. They have been watching us for centuries and are ready to help us with our problems.

Sasquatch are great healers. The healings are the most significant benefits I receive in a relationship with them. I cannot emphasize this enough; they have been life-changing for me. I have become healthier physically, mentally and emotionally. The healings are pretty miraculous.

The Sasquatch People are psychic and can see our spirit. They can see the blocked energy in our bodies and understand the difference made in our health and well-being once a block is cleared out. Sasquatch sees that these blocks are caused by traumatic experiences from living on the third-dimensional plane, Earth.—Sasquatch can literally move the blocks out. After clearing out the trauma (blocks), a world of difference is made in the quality of life for the individual. As I have said before, they are fantastic energy healers. They can help us change our lives.

Time is slipping away. We can no longer afford to be self-centered, looking out for "number one" at all costs. Sasquatch believes we need a complete revision in how we treat one another and the Earth—keeping in mind that some humans live peacefully and are responsible stewards of the Earth. These people walk the talk, as they say. Several of these people have this enlightened knowledge already in place. They are excellent role models for the rest of us and are out there living their life in rhythm with the natural laws of nature. Sadly, they are not your stereotypical American, although they should be!

Americans seem to need a hero to look up to. Unfortunately, American heroes usually pack a gun. The very foundation of America has involved a lot of wars and death—our history books are full of it.

Our time of killing is used up. The negative energy produced by such acts hangs like an unhealthy, psychotic miasma over the world. It affects the natural cycles, rhythms and vibrations of the planet. Everything is affected by this energy—the seasons, flora and fauna, and everything that encompasses the Earth and life upon it.

We are working hard to be happy and productive. Meanwhile, this gloomy cloud of pain, anguish and suffering continuously work against us. At this point, most of us cannot have a happy and productive life because this negative cloud of energy is too large and oppressive. It affects our state of mind, and especially our moods. This cloud of collective negativity will require a higher vibrational energy to transform it, to conquer it by making it neutral. At this point, this negative cloud is festering and becoming more toxic than ever. Millions of people are unhappy and suffering. The energy from suffering collects and adds more to the cloud, causing it to grow larger. We have work to do; we can do it together and win over the negativity. Does a change of scenery sound good right about now? We can start by raising each other. We can intend to raise the vibration of each of our energies and that of others… Also, ask for help, and the Sasquatch or higher spirit beings will come.

We have all lived against nature for too long. We need to start living in support of nature if we want to continue here as a species; we can change this attitude in our next breath. We can begin anew at this very moment—right now. We can mentally rewrite our world story in preparation for a new, excellent storyline of a prosperous, happy life for everyone. It is high time we forget the past and all the negative details. We can rewrite our personal story and pack it with positive words like joy, abundance, love, happy families, clean streams and rivers, clean green energy, thriving animal species and the like. Here is another place we need to keep the list long to allow for unlimited possibilities to manifest in our lives and the lives of others, all others.

At the same time, the Sasquatch People believe we can turn it around quickly by simply owning up to our responsibility for the Earth and releasing our entitled attitude that Earth is ours to do with as we wish. Like Sasquatch says, "Humans are part of the earth, not the center of it."

We see climate change as imminent, but the Sasquatch believe it is still possible to turn it around. Sasquatch urges humans to be open about transforming fear into love. They say as many humans as possible need to be a channel for love. We will raise each other out of the clutches of negativity by becoming channels for love.

When enough humans channel love, we will move in the other direction. We will stop heading for destruction.

We can do this. Love is not a sappy power useful only for Valentine's Day, evidenced only while in a romantic relationship, etc. Love energy is a standard safely kept and guarded by the Sasquatch. The vibration from love energy is the most extraordinary power in this world. It is our most potent energy. When we want something wonderful or exciting to happen in our personal lives, we usually feel the excitement build as we envision ourselves right smack in the middle of our exciting imagined goal. Herein lies the beginning step of how to use the energy effectively. Benevolence, excitement, generosity, fun, beauty and joy are just a few words that define this energy.

This is the beginning stage of allowing our hearts to lead the way. Each of us is unique and has a specific path to follow, which leads us to personal fulfillment. Our courses direct us to an individual blueprint, a plan for a life spent living the way we were meant to live, a path toward satisfaction and happiness. Really, we have lost the art of using this viable tool, love. It almost seems lost forever. Love energy converts negativity into positivity, lack into abundance, fear into confidence, illness into health and so forth.

We can continue taking step after step until we get the hang of it. One first step we can take is to decide to begin using this tool. In your heart, make the intention. Make this the focus of your life, and soon opportunities will flow your way. Practice using this powerful energy. The significant shift I have been writing about will occur when enough people have worked to change their thoughts, words and deeds. The destiny of the world will be changed. It begins when we begin—with ourselves. The Sasquatch believe this is what we are headed toward. They have a lot of confidence in us—They say we will get it done.

They want our thinking to turn around. A large part of the

message from Sasquatch is that we need to rewrite our life scripts about how we see and imagine our world right now and into the future. We need to delete the disaster sections, doomsday fears, and hopeless visions we carry in our hearts. In their place, we must rewrite a new and imaginative script that is developing, thriving and beautiful. Turn your imagination loose and begin imagining the world the way that you would like to see it. Imagine big—*Real Big.*

Thoughts are things. Do you realize that? Imagine your most beautiful world now, and feed it with your heart energy, knowing this is the correct thing to do for your life and the planet. Do it every day. Put it out there to the world and universe, how you need and want the world to be. Make it a most beautiful and fantastic creation.

Try not to place limitations here because humans tend to limit what they believe they deserve. We all deserve to live on a clean and healthy planet with harmonious relationships with one another. We all deserve plenty of food to eat and so forth… We need to change any negative beliefs lodged in our hearts about what we and others deserve. Support from our hearts is crucial. We can forge a great friendship with our hearts. We will become powerful, as positive energy from our hearts is the most powerful energy on Earth.

It is time for our over-thinking brain and ego to take an extended vacation.

Living with thoughts and images that make us excited and happy is powerful, and they create new possibilities for us to enjoy. Even small, positive efforts carry a lot of clout in our lives and the lives of everyone with whom we connect. Each positive action builds up and causes even more changes in the direction our heart is aiming toward—moment by moment, step by step and day by day. It is like tossing a tiny pebble into a clear pond. The ripples radiate over the surface of the water and continue making wave after wave from just one small rock.

We create these ripples daily within our life—only we humans spend a lot of time doing it in reverse. We use low, dense energy that is fear-based, like hate, anger, cheating, jealousy and revenge, for example, thereby creating a destiny headed in an unpleasant direction. —Fear is not a desirable platform from which to orchestrate your life. You may find the results not to your liking, to say the least.

I suspect we have been going down this fearful pathway for so long that we have come to expect doom and gloom. Whatever we have gotten ourselves into, remember that the opposite is just as true—we can get ourselves back out. We can begin by making brand new intentions pointing in the opposite direction. Anything can change. Change is our one and only constant and is the one thing we can truly count on. Change is our best friend—besides our heart, of course.

Sasquatch finds it curious that we live our lives trying to be better than one another and trying to have more and better possessions than everyone else… When we lead our lives competing this way, the very framework is a set-up for one person to win and the other to lose. The Sasquatch thinks it is confusing and can not see the point. It does not lead to happiness, satisfaction or contentment. Instead, it leads to greed, mistrust, alienation and isolation.

Times are changing quickly, and we all need to make progress, each of us. True happiness is shared with everyone. Happiness, in the truest sense, is not something you hoard—it is something you want for everyone. Happiness is when you reach a point where you feel so good you want to share it with others. This is the kind of happiness that lasts. It is the kind of happiness that wells up from within the depths of your soul.

The Sasquatch People are trying to understand human beings now more than ever because they feel responsible as our guides. When asked, I try to answer their questions and explain about humans to them. In my explanations, I usually wind up pointing out that the negative behaviors of humanity stem from fear.

The bottom line for most humans is fear. Our very foundation and premise of existence is fear. Fear has become an underlying guiding principle embedded in almost everything we read and learn through all the various types of schooling and teaching. Our history is loaded with it. It is everywhere. It is in our attitudes, our speech, and our very actions.

Fear is our downfall. We are born learning fear, and we pass this learning down to our children, who continue passing it down to their children, and the passing down continues on to the next generation, and so forth, and so on. Our history shows a tremendous underlayment of fear. It is written everywhere in books of every kind.

Also, our overuse of the word fear has gotten out of control. It is a word that needs to be ejected from the English language. I have been experimenting lately by using replacement words containing a positive spin over the fear-based words I generally use. I have been implanting replacement words like happiness, fun, enjoyment, and how does pleasure sound—for example? I am just testing to see how these positive words change my life. So far, so good—I feel good almost all the time. We no longer need to be loyal to the word fear. Like everything else, fear is replaceable.

However, I see our fear as a symptom of existing in this third-dimensional reality, Earth. Even though the energy has risen to a faster and higher vibrational rate, it may take time for humans to understand how to interact within this new and different energy field. We need to learn how to live well, utilizing the higher frequency. We are all still operating daily as if the energy is still very low. It might take a little time.

One example of how the two energies are different would be that in a third-dimensional reality, your imagination has little power to affect your desires, needs, and the like. Whereas, in the higher and faster vibrations, like the one in which we now breathe and exist, our imagination—plus power from our heart—is the equivalent of being in the driver's seat, steering towards a better reality. We have the energy available to make our world the way we would like to see it. At this time, we can all effect so much change—dramatic change.

Whether or not we are aware of it, we are all up on the quarterdeck aboard the ship of our life, and we are at the helm steering! This is an unprecedented new world in which we all live. We just need to learn how to navigate within it and figure out what direction we want our lives to go.

ONE FINAL MESSAGE FROM Mannie: *"Each human being is magnificent."* He stresses, *"You are capable of greatness, of healing yourselves and healing the planet by coming together and being a true brotherhood [He laughs] or sisterhood. But you have forgotten who you are. That is partly why we are here to help you, to help you understand and remember your true nature."*

Acknowledgments

I WANT TO THANK my editor—Teja Rhae Watson, Two Birds Editing—for advising me to go much deeper into my story, as well as for her experienced, capable editing. I was encouraged by her support and praise of my story—Thank you so much…

I want to thank the telepathic communicator for the excellent work communicating and interpreting between Mannie and me. I really appreciate it—Thank you so very much…

I want to thank my husband for all the countless hours he has spent listening to me and helping me turn my story into a published book.—Thank you for all your tremendous help…

I want to acknowledge all my family members who wholeheartedly supported me in this writing endeavor and who have shared in my excitement throughout this complicated and extraordinary process—Thank you, my family…

I want to thank all my friends and acquaintances who have been the greatest cheerleaders anyone could ever have. Thank you so much for all your incredible support. I will remember it always—Thank you!

—Leanna R Saylor

About the Author

THE AUTHOR IS RETIRED and lives with her husband in the Pacific Northwest, where she spends her time doing artwork, gardening, and traveling with her husband.

www.ingramcontent.com/pod-product-compliance
Lightning Source LLC
Chambersburg PA
CBHW051523120626
46551CB00012B/1055